The INDOOR PLANT SPOTTER
Dr. D.G. Hessayon

1st Impression   400,000

Other Books in the EXPERT Series:
THE FLOWER EXPERT
THE TREE & SHRUB EXPERT
THE HOUSE PLANT EXPERT
THE ROSE EXPERT
THE LAWN EXPERT
THE VEGETABLE EXPERT

Acknowledgements
The author wishes to acknowledge the painstaking work of Gill Jackson and Pauline Dobbs. A special word of thanks is also due to Christopher Chew and Carl Poulsen (Geest), Valerie Day (Rochford) and Eric Gray (Suttons Seeds) for the provision of plants, transparencies and stock lists. Help was received from many other people and organisations, including Joan Hessayon, Angelina Hessayon, Jacqueline Norris, Tony Clements, Challis of York, National Begonia Society, Stuart Low (Enfield), Graham Sinclair Plants, Southdown Flowers, Tesco, Marks & Spencer, The Palm House, Joan Hill, Derek Fox, H. Evans & Son, Holly Gate Cactus Nursery, The Exotic Collection, Roger Grounds, Ivens Orchids, R. H. S. Wisley Garden and Jane Roche.

Photographs and transparencies were received from A-Z Botanical Collection Ltd, Pat Brindley, Bernard Alfieri, Harry Smith Horticultural Photographic Collection, Carleton Photographic, Michael Warren and Dr Yeo.

John Woodbridge provided both artistry and design work. Norman Barber, Henry Barnett and Deborah Achilleos prepared the paintings for this book.

pbi PUBLICATIONS · BRITANNICA HOUSE · WALTHAM CROSS · HERTS · ENGLAND

Contents

Printed and bound in Great Britain by Jarrold & Sons Ltd., Norwich

ISBN 0 903505 21 5

CHAPTER 1
PUTTING A NAME TO YOUR PLANT

The main purpose of this book is to enable you to put a name to each of the plants in your home. It is important for most people to know the identity of the living things in closest contact to them. It obviously can save embarrassment — visitors may walk past the garden flowers but they are sure to ask the name of the unusual 'pretty green thing' growing on the windowsill.

There is a much more practical reason for identifying your house plants. Cultural needs vary greatly, and you can only provide the right conditions if you know what you are growing. Standard textbooks are invaluable for providing information on the requirements and general form of individual plants, but they are often of limited value as a means of identification. Your mystery plant may not be illustrated, and even where it is shown there may be no indication of average leaf or flower size. Descriptions may be glowing, but the key identification features are not highlighted. These are vital if you are trying to name a plant — it is sometimes quite a small feature which separates one species from another.

So in this book the vast array of decorative plants which you are likely to find indoors is divided into numerous groups, each one containing varieties with at least one major feature in common. To start the naming process, carefully look at the growth habit of the plant and measure a few mature leaves (and flowers if present). Turn to pages 2 and 3 and follow the chart which will lead you to the correct group. Search through the plants in this group for the one with the same key features as your specimen.

There is no 'proper' way of classifying indoor plants. The groupings chosen here are entirely artificial and are not based on botanical relationships. They are based instead on physical differences which can be easily spotted by beginner and expert alike. The latin names chosen are the ones most generally used — scientists have a bad habit of inventing strange-sounding new names for old favourites which should be left alone!

This book would be far smaller if it was restricted to the plants which are frequently seen in hall, kitchen and living room. The plan, however, has been to encompass the full span of the words 'indoor plant'. Conservatory plants which may be unsuitable for the living room are included. So are those garden annuals, garden bulbs and outdoor shrubs which make excellent indoor subjects, but are usually omitted from standard books on house plants.

This wide span covers rarities as well as the favourites which have been described over and over again and are seen in every garden centre. Some of these rarities are far too recent to have gained popular acceptance — Breynia, Radermachera and Mikania are examples. Others have been available for many years but are not raised by the major growers. To find them you will have to hunt for a specialist nursery.

Some people may object to the inclusion of rarities which they will never see in High St shops and garden centres. Others may feel that well-known garden plants have no place in a book on indoor plants. The role of this book, however, is not to pass judgements on what is a 'proper' house plant and what is not. It seeks solely to display the range of plants which can be grown indoors and then leaves it to the reader to choose between the commonplace and the out of the ordinary.

KEY TO THE HOUSE PLANT GROUPS

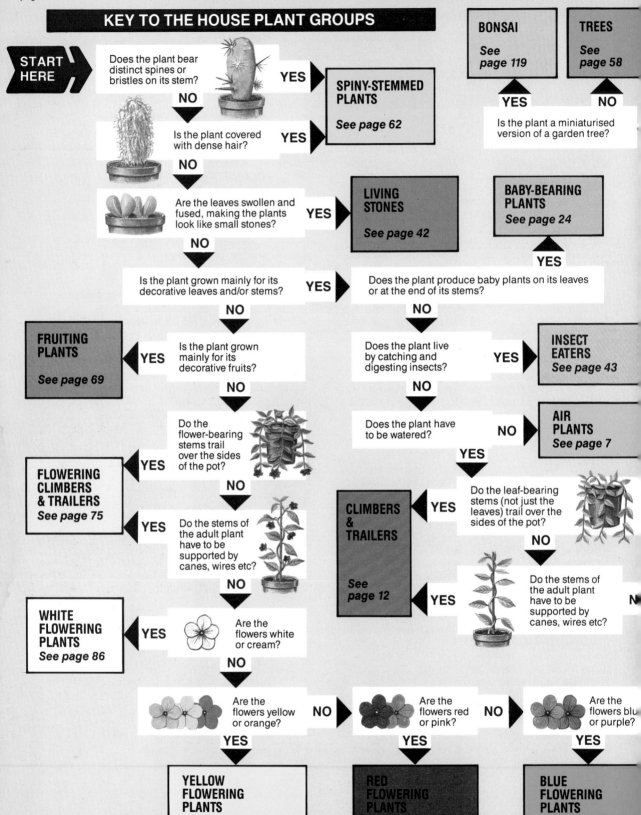

START HERE

Does the plant bear distinct spines or bristles on its stem?
YES → **SPINY-STEMMED PLANTS** See page 62

NO

Is the plant covered with dense hair? **YES** → **SPINY-STEMMED PLANTS** See page 62

NO

Are the leaves swollen and fused, making the plants look like small stones? **YES** → **LIVING STONES** See page 42

NO

Is the plant grown mainly for its decorative leaves and/or stems? **YES** → Does the plant produce baby plants on its leaves or at the end of its stems?

NO

Is the plant grown mainly for its decorative fruits? **YES** → **FRUITING PLANTS** See page 69

NO

Do the flower-bearing stems trail over the sides of the pot? **YES** → **FLOWERING CLIMBERS & TRAILERS** See page 75

NO

Do the stems of the adult plant have to be supported by canes, wires etc? **YES** → **FLOWERING CLIMBERS & TRAILERS** See page 75

NO

Are the flowers white or cream? **YES** → **WHITE FLOWERING PLANTS** See page 86

NO

Are the flowers yellow or orange? **NO** →

YES → **YELLOW FLOWERING PLANTS** See page 88

Are the flowers red or pink? **NO** →

YES → **RED FLOWERING PLANTS** See page 81

Are the flowers blue or purple?

YES → **BLUE FLOWERING PLANTS** See page 84

BONSAI See page 119

TREES See page 58

YES ← **BONSAI** / **NO** → **TREES**

Is the plant a miniaturised version of a garden tree?

BABY-BEARING PLANTS See page 24

YES

Does the plant produce baby plants on its leaves or at the end of its stems?

NO

Does the plant live by catching and digesting insects? **YES** → **INSECT EATERS** See page 43

NO

Does the plant have to be watered? **NO** → **AIR PLANTS** See page 7

YES

Do the leaf-bearing stems (not just the leaves) trail over the sides of the pot? **YES** → **CLIMBERS & TRAILERS** See page 12

NO

Do the stems of the adult plant have to be supported by canes, wires etc? **YES** → **CLIMBERS & TRAILERS** See page 12

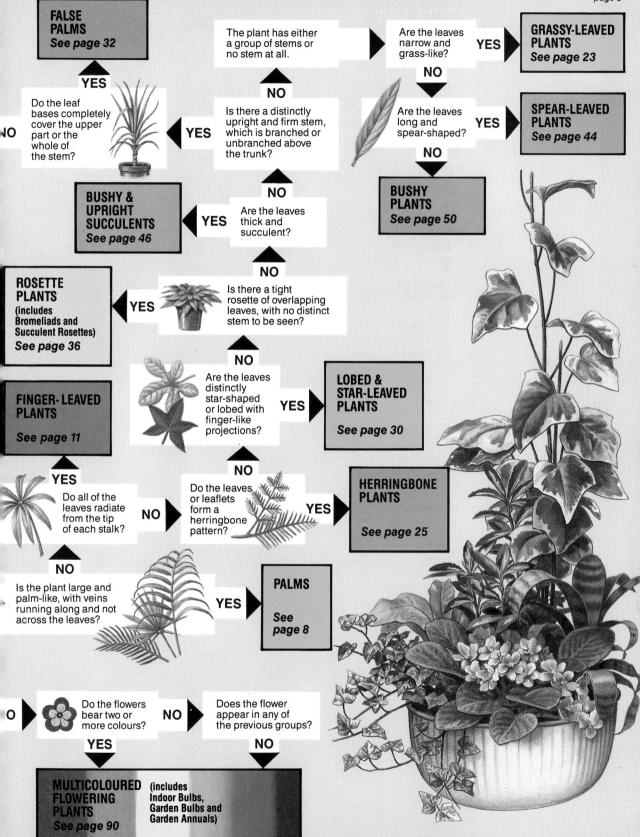

FALSE PALMS
See page 32

YES

Do the leaf bases completely cover the upper part or the whole of the stem?

NO

YES

The plant has either a group of stems or no stem at all.

NO

Is there a distinctly upright and firm stem, which is branched or unbranched above the trunk?

Are the leaves narrow and grass-like?

YES

GRASSY-LEAVED PLANTS
See page 23

NO

Are the leaves long and spear-shaped?

YES

SPEAR-LEAVED PLANTS
See page 44

NO

BUSHY PLANTS
See page 50

NO

BUSHY & UPRIGHT SUCCULENTS
See page 46

YES

Are the leaves thick and succulent?

NO

ROSETTE PLANTS
(includes Bromeliads and Succulent Rosettes)
See page 36

YES

Is there a tight rosette of overlapping leaves, with no distinct stem to be seen?

NO

Are the leaves distinctly star-shaped or lobed with finger-like projections?

YES

LOBED & STAR-LEAVED PLANTS
See page 30

NO

FINGER- LEAVED PLANTS
See page 11

YES

Do all of the leaves radiate from the tip of each stalk?

NO

Do the leaves or leaflets form a herringbone pattern?

YES

HERRINGBONE PLANTS
See page 25

NO

Is the plant large and palm-like, with veins running along and not across the leaves?

YES

PALMS
See page 8

O

Do the flowers bear two or more colours?

NO

Does the flower appear in any of the previous groups?

YES

NO

MULTICOLOURED FLOWERING PLANTS
See page 90

(includes Indoor Bulbs, Garden Bulbs and Garden Annuals)

EXAMPLES OF THE HOUSE PLANT GROUPS

INDOOR BULBS
See page 90

GARDEN ANNUALS
See page 104

BONSAI
See page 119

FLOWERING CLIMBERS
See page 75

GARDEN BULBS
See page 94

AIR PLANTS
See page 7

INSECT EATERS
See page 43

SUCCULENT ROSETTES
See page 39

TRAILERS
See page 12

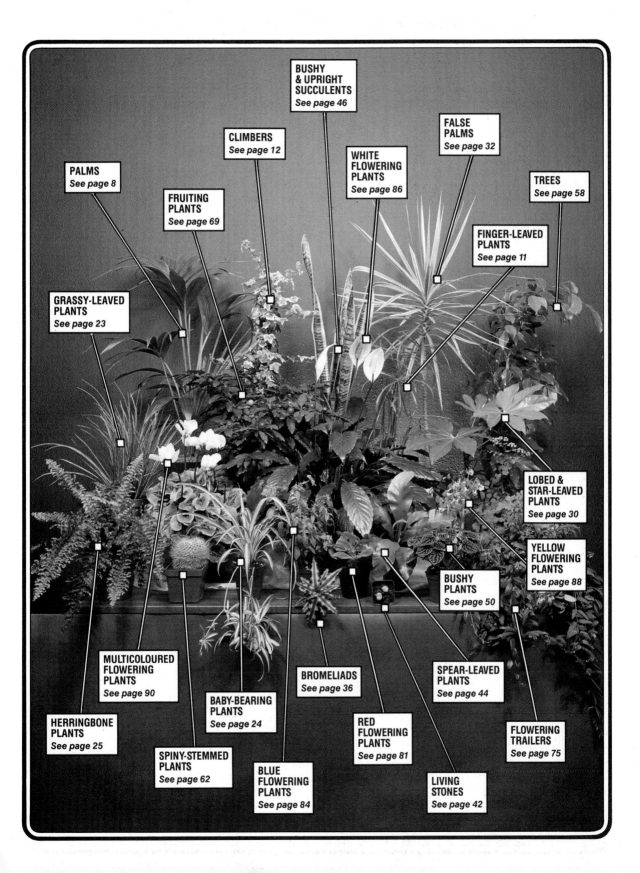

BUSHY & UPRIGHT SUCCULENTS
See page 46

FALSE PALMS
See page 32

CLIMBERS
See page 12

WHITE FLOWERING PLANTS
See page 86

TREES
See page 58

PALMS
See page 8

FRUITING PLANTS
See page 69

FINGER-LEAVED PLANTS
See page 11

GRASSY-LEAVED PLANTS
See page 23

LOBED & STAR-LEAVED PLANTS
See page 30

YELLOW FLOWERING PLANTS
See page 88

BUSHY PLANTS
See page 50

MULTICOLOURED FLOWERING PLANTS
See page 90

BROMELIADS
See page 36

SPEAR-LEAVED PLANTS
See page 44

HERRINGBONE PLANTS
See page 25

BABY-BEARING PLANTS
See page 24

RED FLOWERING PLANTS
See page 81

FLOWERING TRAILERS
See page 75

SPINY-STEMMED PLANTS
See page 62

BLUE FLOWERING PLANTS
See page 84

LIVING STONES
See page 42

CHAPTER 2

FOLIAGE HOUSE PLANTS

Foliage house plants are grown for the beauty or novelty of their leaves or for the attractive shape of their stems. A few of them bear flowers indoors — usually insignificant but quite showy in the case of some succulents. With all of them, however, it is the foliage or the general growth habit which earns them a place in the home.

Each year about 50 million house plants are bought, but less than half are foliage types. Despite the predominance of flowering plants in the shops, it is the foliage group which you are most likely to find growing in the home. The reason for this odd fact is that most flowering pot plants are bought for temporary display, to bloom for a month or two before being thrown away. Foliage house plants on the other hand are nearly always bought as permanent residents, to be kept for years in the home.

The indoor gardener generally uses foliage house plants to provide an evergreen and permanent background. To this display are added flowering plants to provide splashes of bright colour. This does not mean that the background of foliage house plants needs to be dull or uniformly green. There is an enormous range of leaf size, texture and colour. Sizes range from the ⅛ in. long leaves of the Artillery Plant and Selaginella to the 2 ft leaves of Dracaena and Monstera. Colours vary from the near-white of Aglaonema Silver King and Scindapsus aureus Marble Queen to the near-black of Philodendron melanochrysum and Aeonium arboreum atropurpureum Schwarzkopf.

The last-named variety illustrates the tongue-twisting nature of many latin names. Wherever possible common names are given in addition to latin names — in practice a mixture of latin and common names is used to describe the plants in our home. This is illustrated by the list of the favourites which dominate the foliage house plant scene — Ivy, Monstera, Philodendron scandens, Parlour and Kentia Palms, Adiantum and Boston Ferns, Scindapsus, Rubber Plant, Dracaena, Yucca, Caladium, Rhoicissus and Cissus Vines, Tradescantia, Chlorophytum and Mother-in-Law's Tongue.

Your mystery plant may or may not be one of the popular group listed above. Begin by studying the growth habit — do the stems trail over the pot or do they stand upright without support? Look at the shape of a mature leaf — is it oval, spear-shaped, lobed, herringbone-like, etc? Measure its size and note its colour — check if the underside is a different colour. Texture may be important — is it fleshy or is the surface unusual in any way? The presence of a velvety, waxy, warty or hairy surface may be important for identification. The arrangement of the leaves is a most important factor — are they borne as a stemless rosette, does a crown of foliage clothe a short stem or is there a series of leaves on thin stalks attached to a bare trunk?

Armed with these facts you will have been led to the correct section of this chapter, and you should be able to find the correct name by comparing your plant with the examples decribed.

If you cannot find it, consider the following questions. Is it a flowering or fruiting plant which has not yet reached the stage for identification? If so, wait until the flowers or fruit appear and then use the chart on pages 2-3. Is the plant an immature one or does it have a growth habit which is on the borderline between two groups? If so, look up the alternative section. Finally, is it a variety of a popular species? It would not be possible to illustrate every Ivy, Begonia rex, Coleus, Croton etc here — all that can be shown is a selection of popular varieties.

Air Plants

This chapter on foliage house plants contains many, many old friends but it begins with a most unusual group — the Air Plants. These are the Grey Tillandsias, which differ from their normal green relatives by bearing absorbent furry scales on their foliage. These scales take up water from humid air, and obtain nutrients from air-borne dust — they literally live on air! The commonest species is Tillandsia usneoides — the familiar Spanish Moss which hangs from trees in the warmer regions of America. Until recently they were virtually unknown as house plants in Britain, but you can now find several species for sale at large garden centres. These plants are stuck on coral, shells, driftwood, etc — they are not planted in compost. Four popular Air Plants are shown below — others include T. aeranthos, T. butzii, T. plumosa and T. bulbosa. The leaves around the flowers may change colour and provide a long-lasting bright display, but the blooms themselves last for only a few days.

Tillandsia ionantha forms a compact rosette of arching silvery leaves. It grows only a couple of inches high, and the inner foliage turns red when the stalkless violet flowers appear.

Tillandsia caput-medusae is perhaps the most popular of all the Air Plants. Thick and twisted leaves arise from a bulbous base. The red bracts and blue flowers are very showy.

Tillandsia juncea is a long-leaved species — rush-like foliage spreads outwards and a single flower-stalk bears the terminal blooms well above the heart of the plant.

Tillandsia argentea is a silvery species — the short leaves spread untidily outwards as the plant develops. The flower-stalk also bends and twists, bearing blue or red flowers.

Palms

You must forget the image of tropical outdoor palms bathed in hot sunshine if you want to recognise and successfully grow these elegant plants indoors. As house plants the trunks are usually small or absent — they are grown for their attractive divided leaves known as fronds. Do not prune palms and never cut off a developing frond — only old and brown ones should be removed.

Palms were for a time rejected as being symbols of the Victorian parlour, but they have begun to regain their popularity. Bearing in mind their exotic appearance and natural habitat, most are surprisingly easy to grow. Many will tolerate some shade and will thrive in cool conditions as well as in centrally-heated rooms. Unfortunately they are expensive — the cause is their slow-growing nature. This means that they will not quickly outgrow the allotted space in your home, but it does also mean that they are costly to raise. Still, a large palm is a sound investment if you want a striking specimen plant for a large room.

There are several groups to choose from — the Feather Palms, the Fan Palms, the Fishtails and so on. The Feather Palms are the most popular.

● FAN PALMS

Trachycarpus fortunei

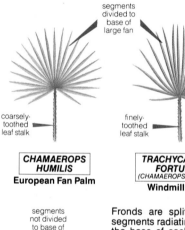

segments divided to base of large fan

coarsely-toothed leaf stalk

CHAMAEROPS HUMILIS
European Fan Palm

finely-toothed leaf stalk

TRACHYCARPUS FORTUNEI
(CHAMAEROPS EXCELSA)
Windmill Palm

segments not divided to base of large fan

drooping tips

toothed leaf stalk

LIVISTONA CHINENSIS
(LATANIA BORBONICA)
Chinese Fan Palm

segments not divided to base of large fan

coarsely-toothed leaf stalk

fibrous threads

WASHINGTONIA FILIFERA
Desert Fan Palm

Fronds are split into numerous segments radiating from a point at the base of each frond — these segments may be entirely or only partly divided. The leaf stalks are long, up to 2 ft or more, and are generally toothed. The Fan Palms are not widely grown as house plants — the large leaves can be dramatic in the right situation but have none of the graceful effect associated with palms. Some are easy — **Chamaerops humilis** (the only native European palm) is quite hardy indoors, but others are difficult to grow — **Washingtonia filifera** is short lived. The large-leaved ones are too wide-spreading for the average room — it is only the smaller-leaved **Rhapis excelsa** with its upright stems which is widely sold.

segments divided to base of small fan — leaflets 8 in. long

RHAPIS EXCELSA
Little Lady Palm

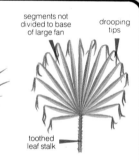

● FEATHER PALMS

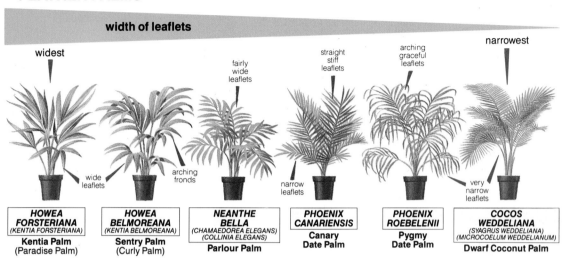

width of leaflets

widest — narrowest

widest

wide leaflets

fairly wide leaflets

arching fronds

straight stiff leaflets

arching graceful leaflets

narrow leaflets

very narrow leaflets

| HOWEA FORSTERIANA (KENTIA FORSTERIANA) Kentia Palm (Paradise Palm) | HOWEA BELMOREANA (KENTIA BELMOREANA) Sentry Palm (Curly Palm) | NEANTHE BELLA (CHAMAEDOREA ELEGANS) (COLLINIA ELEGANS) Parlour Palm | PHOENIX CANARIENSIS Canary Date Palm | PHOENIX ROEBELENII Pygmy Date Palm | COCOS WEDDELIANA (SYAGRUS WEDDELIANA) (MICROCOELUM WEDDELIANUM) Dwarf Coconut Palm |

Fronds are divided on either side of the midrib into leaflets — these leaflets may be soft and drooping or stiff and erect. **Neanthe bella,** the most widely grown of all indoor palms, belongs to this group. It may be listed as **Collinia elegans** or **Chamaedorea elegans Bella** in the textbooks, but all these names refer to the old favourite Parlour Palm which is usually bought as a 6–12 in. specimen. After a few years it will reach its adult height of about 2 ft and tiny yellow flowers and small fruit appear if grown in good light. The dwarf nature of Neanthe makes it ideal for small rooms and bottle gardens — for a much bolder display the usual choice is one of the Howea (Kentia) palms. These are the traditional Palm Court plants which grow up to 8 ft tall. It is not too easy to distinguish between the 2 species — **Howea forsteriana** is the British favourite and is quicker growing but less arching than **H. belmoreana.**

The true Date Palm (**Phoenix dactylifera**) is less attractive though quicker growing than the species of Phoenix sold as house plants — **P. canariensis** (6 ft) and **P. roebelenii** (3 ft). The true Coconut Palm (**Cocos nucifera**) unfortunately dies after a couple of years indoors. Its near relative **Cocos weddeliana** (more correctly **Syagrus weddeliana**) is sold as a house plant and is thought by some experts to be the most attractive of all the indoor palms. But it has none of the hardiness of the popular types and needs the warmth and humidity of a conservatory.

Howea forsteriana

Neanthe bella

● SAGO PALMS

CYCAS REVOLUTA

Sago Palm

ball-like base

The Sago Palms (cycads) are distinctly palm-like in appearance but they are not closely related to the true palms. You will find only one species at the garden centre — **Cycas revoluta.** It is an extremely slow-growing plant, putting out just one leaf per year. In time an attractive, dark green rosette of stiff arching foliage is formed — mature height 2 ft.

Cycas revoluta

● FISHTAIL PALMS

CARYOTA MITIS

Burmese Fishtail Palm

wedge-shaped leaflets

The Fishtail Palms get their name from the shape of the leaflets, which are about 6 in. long and 4 in. wide. **Caryota mitis** is the favourite one — lots of ragged-edged leaflets on arching fronds. **C. urens** (Wine Fishtail Palm) is less popular and less attractive — its leaflets are more triangular but there are fewer of them. Both types form stems — mature height 6–8 ft.

Caryota urens

● CANE PALMS

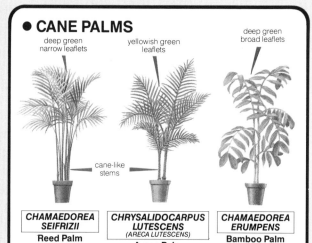

deep green narrow leaflets

yellowish green leaflets

deep green broad leaflets

cane-like stems

CHAMAEDOREA SEIFRIZII

Reed Palm

CHRYSALIDOCARPUS LUTESCENS
(ARECA LUTESCENS)

Areca Palm
(Butterfly Palm)

CHAMAEDOREA ERUMPENS

Bamboo Palm

A small group of palms produce tall reed-like stems which look rather like bamboo canes when mature. These plants are popular with interior decorators in the U.S., providing bold focal points for large rooms. Reed and Bamboo Palms can grow 6–10 ft tall under good conditions and the fronds of the Areca Palm may reach 3 ft or more. **Rhapis excelsa** (page 8) and the closely related **R. humilis** are sometimes called Bamboo Palms as their slender stems can grow 5–7 ft high.

Chrysalidocarpus lutescens

Finger-leaved Plants

A small group of house plants which can be easily identified by their 'umbrella' leaves. Several long leaves, leaflets or leaf-like structures radiate like the spokes of an umbrella from the top of each stalk. Plants range in height from 1–8 ft.

● SAW-EDGED LEAVES

Dizygotheca elegantissima

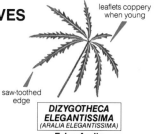

leaflets coppery when young

saw-toothed edge

DIZYGOTHECA ELEGANTISSIMA
(ARALIA ELEGANTISSIMA)
False Aralia
(Finger Aralia)

D. elegantissima is the popular species — delicate in both appearance and constitution. This plant can grow up to 6 ft high, but the dark green leaves lose their lacy effect in old specimens. **D. veitchii** has wider leaves with wavy (not serrated) edges.

● NARROW LEAVES

palm-like leaves

CYPERUS DIFFUSUS
Umbrella Plant

grass-like leaves

CYPERUS ALTERNIFOLIUS
Umbrella Plant

thread-like leaves

CYPERUS PAPYRUS
Papyrus

Cyperus alternifolius

Cyperus bears reed-like stems, each topped with a crown of grassy leaves or leaf-like structures. **C. papyrus** (6–8 ft), the source of both paper and Moses' cradle in biblical times — too tall and difficult for most homes. The popular ones are **C. diffusus** (1–2 ft) and **C. alternifolius** (3–4 ft). C. alternifolius has two interesting varieties — **C. alternifolius gracilis** (1½ ft, dark green leaves) and **C. alternifolius variegatus** (3 ft, white-striped leaves).

● BROAD LEAVES

Heptapleurum arboricola variegata

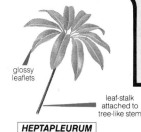

glossy leaflets

HEPTAPLEURUM ARBORICOLA
Parasol Plant

Less popular and more slender than Schefflera. Remove growing point for a quick-growing bush or stake and leave unpinched to produce a 6 ft unbranched tree. Named varieties are available — **Hayata** (greyish leaves), **Hong Kong** (dwarf growing) and **variegata** (yellow-splashed leaves).

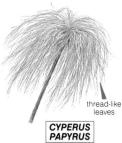

leathery, glossy leaflets

leaf-stalk attached to tree-like stem

SCHEFFLERA ACTINOPHYLLA
(BRASSAIA ACTINOPHYLLA)
Umbrella Tree

Attractive bush when young, tall (6–8 ft) tree when mature — widely used as a specimen plant. Number of leaflets per stalk increases from 4 to 12 with age. Does not flower under room conditions.

Schefflera actinophylla

Climbers & Trailers

An extremely important group — more than half the foliage plants we buy are either climbers or trailers. There is no clear-cut dividing line between these two types. Some plants, such as Monstera deliciosa, are always provided with upright support and are therefore invariably grown as climbers. A number of others, such as Helxine soleirolii and Selaginella uncinata, are always grown as trailers. But the remainder can be treated either way — trained to grow upwards as a climber or left to sprawl or trail over the pot.

Climbers come in two forms. There are the self-supporting plants, clinging to wires or canes by means of tendrils. The remainder are self supporting in their natural habitat but have no means of holding on to sticks or strings when grown as house plants — tying is therefore essential.

One point to remember when identifying a young plant — juvenile stems usually grow upright for a time before the trailing habit or need for support becomes apparent.

● HEART-LEAVED CLIMBERS

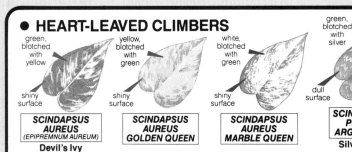

green, blotched with yellow — shiny surface

SCINDAPSUS AUREUS (EPIPREMNUM AUREUM)
Devil's Ivy (Golden Pothos)

yellow, blotched with green — shiny surface

SCINDAPSUS AUREUS GOLDEN QUEEN

white, blotched with green — shiny surface

SCINDAPSUS AUREUS MARBLE QUEEN

green, blotched with silver — thin white line around edge — dull surface

SCINDAPSUS PICTUS ARGYRAEUS
Silver Vine

Scindapsus aureus

Devil's Ivy is similar to but more colourful than the Sweetheart Plant. The easiest to grow is **S. aureus** — it can be treated as a trailer or climber, reaching 6 ft or more under good conditions. The near-white and near-yellow varieties are not easy to grow. Usual leaf size of S. aureus is 4–6 in. — **S. pictus** is smaller and more difficult.

Philodendron scandens

shiny surface — bronzy at first, dark green later

PHILODENDRON SCANDENS (PHILODENDRON OXYCARDIUM)
Sweetheart Plant

The Sweetheart Plant (Heart-leaf Philodendron) is extremely popular and is one of the easiest plants to grow. Thin stems bear 3–5 in. shiny leaves. Grow as a trailer — pinch out tips to keep plant bushy. Or grow as a climber — retain aerial roots and use a moss stick (page 13) for maximum effect.

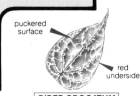

puckered surface — red underside

PIPER CROCATUM
Ornamental Pepper

The waxy, dappled leaves (3–5 in. long) make Ornamental Pepper much more eye-catching than the Sweetheart Plant, but it is much more difficult to find in the shops and to grow successfully indoors. Two varieties are available — **P. crocatum** (underside dark red) and **P. ornatum** (underside light green). Both may be grown as climbers or trailers.

Piper crocatum

● LARGE-LEAVED PHILODENDRONS

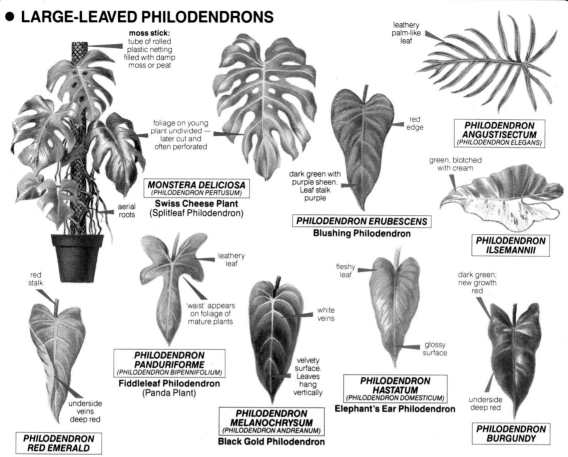

moss stick:
tube of rolled
plastic netting
filled with damp
moss or peat

foliage on young
plant undivided —
later cut and
often perforated

aerial
roots

MONSTERA DELICIOSA
(PHILODENDRON PERTUSUM)
Swiss Cheese Plant
(Splitleaf Philodendron)

leathery
palm-like
leaf

**PHILODENDRON
ANGUSTISECTUM**
(PHILODENDRON ELEGANS)

red
edge

dark green with
purple sheen.
Leaf stalk
purple

PHILODENDRON ERUBESCENS
Blushing Philodendron

green, blotched
with cream

**PHILODENDRON
ILSEMANNII**

red
stalk

leathery
leaf

'waist' appears
on foliage of
mature plants

.**PHILODENDRON
PANDURIFORME**
(PHILODENDRON BIPENNIFOLIUM)
Fiddleleaf Philodendron
(Panda Plant)

white
veins

velvety
surface.
Leaves
hang
vertically

**PHILODENDRON
MELANOCHRYSUM**
(PHILODENDRON ANDREANUM)
Black Gold Philodendron

fleshy
leaf

glossy
surface

**PHILODENDRON
HASTATUM**
(PHILODENDRON DOMESTICUM)
Elephant's Ear Philodendron

dark green;
new growth
red

underside
deep red

**PHILODENDRON
BURGUNDY**

underside
veins
deep red

**PHILODENDRON
RED EMERALD**

Philodendron melanochrysum

The Philodendrons and closely-related Monsteras live in the tropical rain-forests of America. In their native home they grow 60 ft or more, clinging to the trunks of trees by means of aerial roots. Indoors they will grow 6–15 ft if the aerial roots are not removed.

These plants are the most spectacular of all the house plant climbers. A moss stick is the ideal support and the leaves of some varieties exceed 2 ft in length. The leathery foliage varies widely in shape (entire to deeply cut), colour (pale green to rich red) and texture (glossy to velvety). Some grow quickly — **Philodendron imbe** can increase by 7 ft in 2–3 years, whereas **P. Burgundy** will grow less than 1 ft in the same length of time.

The old favourite of the group is, of course, **Monstera deliciosa**. With care, leaves measuring 2 ft across will be produced — a compact variety (**borsigiana**) is available and so is a cream-blotched form (**variegata**). The general foliage pattern for the large-leaved Philodendrons is a 6–15 in. arrow-shaped leaf with a glossy surface. Popular varieties include **P. hastatum** and its more branching hybrid **P. Tuxla**. **P. erubescens** and its hybrids such as **Red Emerald** and **Burgundy** are more colourful, and the dramatic two are the velvety **P. melanochrysum** and the variegated **P. ilsemannii**.

Philodendron Red Emerald

● TRUE IVIES

stems not self supporting

leaves not succulent

HEDERA HELIX
English Ivy

HEDERA HELIX CHICAGO

HEDERA HELIX LITTLE EVA

HEDERA HELIX CRISTATA
Parsley Ivy

HEDERA HELIX GLACIER

HEDERA HELIX LUTZII

HEDERA HELIX JUBILEE
Goldheart Ivy

HEDERA HELIX SCUTIFOLIA

HEDERA HELIX SAGITTAEFOLIA
Needlepoint Ivy

HEDERA HELIX IVALACE
Lacyleaf Ivy

HEDERA CANARIENSIS GLOIRE DE MARENGO
Canary Island Ivy

HEDERA HELIX MARMORATA

The general form of ivy needs no description — it is grown in homes throughout Europe and America. Less well known, however, is the extent of the variations on the basic pattern. Nearly all the True Ivies are varieties of the Common or English Ivy (**Hedera helix**) which bears characteristically lobed leaves. These varieties range in leaf form from simple shields (**scutifolia**) to long-pointed stars (**sagittaefolia**). Edges are smooth or ruffled, and colours vary from simple green to complex mixtures of white, cream, grey, green and yellow.

The largest-leaved ivy is **H. canariensis**. The green-leaved species is not popular — the type seen everywhere is the variegated **Gloire de Marengo**. Most True Ivies can be grown as either climbers or trailers — for a compact ground cover choose a small-leaved variety and pinch out the growing tips 2 or 3 times each year.

Hedera helix Golden Harald

Hedera helix Kholibra

Hedera canariensis Gloire de Marengo

● OTHER IVIES

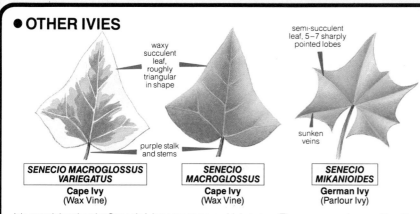

waxy succulent leaf, roughly triangular in shape

purple stalk and stems

semi-succulent leaf, 5–7 sharply pointed lobes

sunken veins

| **SENECIO MACROGLOSSUS VARIEGATUS** Cape Ivy (Wax Vine) | **SENECIO MACROGLOSSUS** Cape Ivy (Wax Vine) | **SENECIO MIKANIOIDES** German Ivy (Parlour Ivy) |

It is surprising that the Senecio Ivies are not more widely grown. They are more vigorous than the True Ivies and are less affected by the warm and dry conditions in a centrally-heated room in winter. Small daisy-like flowers appear if kept in a well-lit spot. They are tall growing — pinch out tips to induce bushiness. **Senecio macroglossus** is rarely grown — you are more likely to find the yellow-blotched form **(variegatus).**

Senecio macroglossus variegatus

Hemigraphis alternata

purple metallic sheen

stalk and underside wine red

| **HEMIGRAPHIS ALTERNATA** *(HEMIGRAPHIS COLORATA)* Red Ivy |

A rarity on both sides of the Atlantic and not worth searching for unless you can provide winter warmth. Despite its name, this plant is quite different to a True Ivy — growth is limited to 1–1½ ft and the 3 in. leaves are oval. **H. exotica** has puckered leaves.

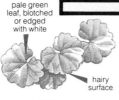

pale green leaf, blotched or edged with white

hairy surface

| **GLECHOMA HEDERACEA VARIEGATA** Ground Ivy |

You will have difficulty in finding this one, but it is a useful ground cover or trailer for hanging baskets. The stems grow quickly — cut back occasionally to maintain bushiness. Leaves are about 1 in. across — blue flowers appear but are small. Sometimes listed as **Nepeta hederacea.**

Glechoma hederacea variegata

Plectranthus australis

prominent white veins

underside and leaf edge rosy-purple

broad white edge

hairy surface

waxy dark green leaf

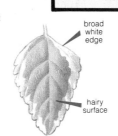

| **PLECTRANTHUS OERTENDAHLII** Swedish Ivy | **PLECTRANTHUS COLEOIDES MARGINATUS** Swedish Ivy | **PLECTRANTHUS AUSTRALIS** Swedish Ivy |

It is a pity that Plectranthus has not become popular. The advantages of these creeping plants as ground cover and for clothing the edges of pots and hanging baskets are well known in Scandinavia. Hence the common name (Swedish Ivy) for all the trailing varieties — plants which flourish in dry air where True Ivies would fail and with the added bonus of occasional flowers. The foliage of the most popular type **(P. oertendahlii)** is especially colourful. Its leaves measure 1 in. across — the largest are borne by **P. coleoides marginatus** (2–2½ in.).

● VINES

tendrils present

glossy surface

leaflets 6 in. long

quick-growing stems

underside furry

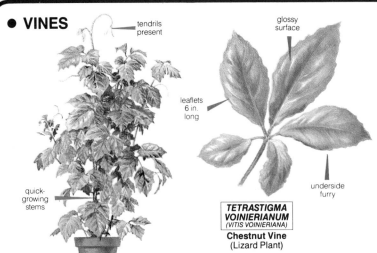

TETRASTIGMA VOINIERIANUM
(VITIS VOINIERIANA)
Chestnut Vine
(Lizard Plant)

Tetrastigma voinierianum

green, blotched with yellow, cream or red

The True Vines are all members of the Grape family — they climb by means of tendrils and two of them (Grape Ivy and Kangaroo Vine) are extremely popular and easy to grow. **Tetrastigma voinierianum** is much less popular — it is an extremely rampant grower and is not really happy away from the conservatory or greenhouse. **Ampelopsis brevipedunculata** is even less common — its habit of losing its leaves in winter is a serious disadvantage. **Cissus antarctica** is a great favourite for covering screens or other large areas, growing about 10 ft tall and clothing the supports with its leathery leaves. The quick-growing **Cissus striata** is generally used as a trailer. The tender Cissus is **C. discolor** — the unusual one is **C. gongylodes** which bears red aerial roots. **Rhoicissus rhomboidea** is perhaps the most tolerant of all house plants and is seen everywhere. For something a little different choose the variety **Ellen Danica** (lobed leaflets) or **Jubilee** (large, dark green leaflets).

AMPELOPSIS BREVIPEDUNCULATA
(VITIS HETEROPHYLLA VARIEGATA)
Virginia Creeper

Cissus antarctica

green, blotched with silver and pale purple. Red tendrils

leaf 4 in. long

glossy surface

leaflets 1 in. long

leaflets pink when young

leaf 6 in. long

underside red

CISSUS ANTARCTICA
Kangaroo Vine

CISSUS STRIATA

CISSUS DISCOLOR
Begonia Vine

glossy surface with brown edge. Underside brown and furry

new growth silvery

leaflets deeply lobed

leaf 8 in. wide

leaflets 2 in. long

leaflets 2½ in. long

RHOICISSUS CAPENSIS
(CISSUS CAPENSIS)
Cape Grape
(Evergreen Grape Vine)

RHOICISSUS RHOMBOIDEA
(CISSUS RHOMBIFOLIA)
Grape Ivy
(Natal Vine)

RHOICISSUS RHOMBOIDEA ELLEN DANICA
Mermaid Vine

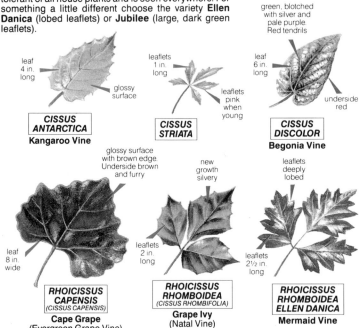

Rhoicissus rhomboidea Ellen Danica

● GOOSEFOOT CLIMBERS

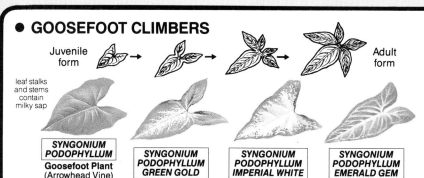

Juvenile form → → → Adult form

leaf stalks and stems contain milky sap

SYNGONIUM PODOPHYLLUM
Goosefoot Plant (Arrowhead Vine)

SYNGONIUM PODOPHYLLUM GREEN GOLD

SYNGONIUM PODOPHYLLUM IMPERIAL WHITE

SYNGONIUM PODOPHYLLUM EMERALD GEM

Syngonium podophyllum Emerald Gem

The Goosefoots or Syngoniums are closely related to the climbing Philodendrons and require the same growing conditions. They are sometimes sold under the name **Nephthytis podophyllum**. The variegated types are the popular ones, ranging from almost entirely green to practically all-white or yellow. The young leaves are the most attractive, being eared and not divided into separate leaflets. Maintain the production of this juvenile foliage by removing the tips of climbing stems as they appear.

● WANDERING JEWS

spear-shaped leaves which clasp the stem

pale purple sap
leaf 2–3 in. long
underside pale purple

TRADESCANTIA FLUMINENSIS VARIEGATA

shiny surface
leaf 2–2½ in. long
colourless sap

TRADESCANTIA ALBIFLORA ALBOVITTATA

dull surface
leaf 3–4 in. long
leaves borne on hairy stems
underside purple

TRADESCANTIA BLOSSFELDIANA VARIEGATA

dull surface
leaf 1–1½ in. long
underside purple

CALLISIA ELEGANS
Striped Inch Plant

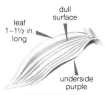

glistening surface
leaf 2 in. long
underside purple
green, banded with silver

ZEBRINA PENDULA
Silvery Inch Plant

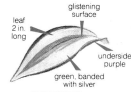

glistening surface
leaf 2½ in. long
underside purple

ZEBRINA PENDULA PURPUSII
Bronze Inch Plant

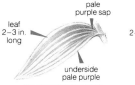

Wandering Jew, Wandering Sailor, Spiderwort, Inch Plant — all describe Tradescantia and a couple of close relatives. **T. fluminensis** is perhaps the most popular — the varieties grown are **variegata** (cream striped) and **Quicksilver** (white striped). **T. albiflora** is similar, but neither the sap nor the underside of the foliage is mauve. The usual varieties are **albovittata** (white striped), **tricolor** (white and mauve striped) and **aurea** (yellow with green stripes). **T. blossfeldiana variegata** is the popular large-leaved type.

Zebrina is closely related but more colourful — the showpiece variety is **Z. pendula quadricolor** with its green, silver, pink and red leaves. **Callisia elegans** bears fleshy foliage, dull green and white above — deep purple below.

Callisia elegans

Tradescantia fluminensis Quicksilver

Zebrina pendula quadricolor

● OTHER CLIMBERS & TRAILERS

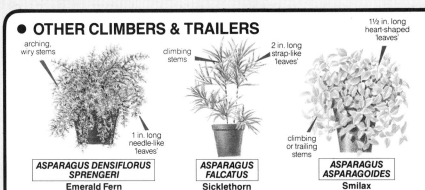

arching, wiry stems

1 in. long needle-like 'leaves'

ASPARAGUS DENSIFLORUS SPRENGERI
Emerald Fern

climbing stems

2 in. long strap-like 'leaves'

ASPARAGUS FALCATUS
Sicklethorn

1½ in. long heart-shaped 'leaves'

climbing or trailing stems

ASPARAGUS ASPARAGOIDES
Smilax

Asparagus densiflorus sprengeri

Several types of Asparagus are grown as house plants — they are often called Asparagus Ferns but are not ferns at all. The climbers and trailers are shown here — the most popular one is **A. densiflorus sprengeri**. The 'leaves' of **A. falcatus** are larger and the stems grow 3 ft high. Smilax is a florist-shop favourite, its shiny foliage remaining fresh for a long time after cutting. Asparagus 'leaves' are really modified branchlets.

Ceropegia woodii

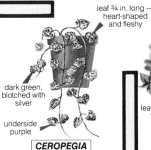

leaf ¾ in. long — heart-shaped and fleshy

dark green, blotched with silver

underside purple

CEROPEGIA WOODII
Rosary Vine
(String of Hearts)

An unusual succulent for a hanging basket or a pot standing on a shelf. The wiry stems grow about 3 ft long. It is an easy plant to grow, but the foliage is unfortunately sparse and the 1 in. tubular flowers are insignificant.

leaf 1 in. long fleshy and covered with fur

underside purple

CYANOTIS KEWENSIS
Teddy Bear Vine

Close relatives of the popular Tradescantia, from which they differ by bearing densely hairy leaves. **Cyanotis kewensis** foliage bears rusty brown hairs — the leaves of **C. somaliensis** (Pussy Ears) are larger and the hairs are pale grey.

Cyanotis somaliensis

Dichorisandra reginae

green, blotched and striped with silver

leaf 5 in. long

underside purple

DICHORISANDRA REGINAE
Queen's Spiderwort

Dichorisandra looks like an enlarged version of the ever-popular Tradescantia (page 17). You will not find this plant at your local garden centre — you will have to search the list of a specialist supplier to find one. Bushy at first, but the fully-grown stems (2 ft) need support.

shiny surface

leaf 7 in. long

FATSHEDERA LIZEI
Ivy Tree

This hybrid of Hedera and Fatsia was introduced about 70 years ago. The stems can reach 6 ft or more. Support is needed, or you can pinch out the tips and grow it as a bush. The white-blotched form (**variegata**) is more difficult to grow.

Fatshedera lizei variegata

leaf 1 in. long

thin heart-shaped leaves

thin wiry stem

FICUS PUMILA
(FICUS REPENS)
Creeping Fig

leaf ½ in. long

thin heart-shaped leaves

thin wiry stem

FICUS PUMILA MINIMA
Creeping Fig

leaf 3 in. long

wiry stem

thin wiry stem

leathery pointed leaves

FICUS RADICANS VARIEGATA
Trailing Fig

The word 'Ficus' conjures up a picture of Rubber Plants and other tree-like specimens, but there are two lowly species which are useful as trailers or as climbers if provided with support. **Ficus pumila** produces a dense green carpet and is one of the best of all indoor ground covers — the stems will cling to any damp surface and so it is an excellent climbing subject for a moss stick (see page 13). The variety **minima** has smaller leaves and **variegata** has white-spotted foliage. **F. radicans** has larger leaves with wavy edges — the popular type is the cream-edged **variegata**.

Ficus pumila

leaf 2 in. long

olive green, veined with deep pink

FITTONIA VERSCHAFFELTII
Painted Net Leaf

leaf 1 in. long

green, veined with white

FITTONIA ARGYRONEURA NANA
Snakeskin Plant

leaf 2 in. long

green, veined with white

FITTONIA ARGYRONEURA
Silver Net Leaf

Fittonia is easily recognised — the leaves bear a network of white, pink or red veins. This pattern is responsible for all the common names — Net Plant, Lace Leaf, Snakeskin Plant and so on. The large-leaved **Fittonia verschaffeltii** has pink veins — for bright red veins choose the variety **pearcei**. The white-veined **F. argyroneura** is even more distinctive, but both are difficult to grow under ordinary room conditions. Choose instead the robust miniature **F. argyroneura nana**.

Fittonia argyroneura nana

dark green, covered with purple hairs

leaf 3 in. long

GYNURA SARMENTOSA
Velvet Plant

round leaves on pinkish stems

leaf ⅕ in. long

HELXINE SOLEIROLII
Mind Your Own Business
(Baby's Tears)

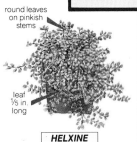

Gynura sarmentosa is a popular trailer, especially for hanging baskets. The foliage has a velvety look — gleaming purple in bright light. **G. aurantiaca** has larger leaves, but it is more upright and less attractive. The flowers are evil-smelling — remove them as they appear.

The mossy mounds of **Helxine soleirolii (Soleirolia soleirolii)** were being used for ground cover in conservatories long before the start of the present boom in house plants. It is extremely easy to propagate — just pull off a clump of the thread-like stems and push into a pot of compost.

Gynura sarmentosa

Helxine soleirolii argentea

● OTHER CLIMBERS & TRAILERS continued

Breynia nivosa roseopicta

BREYNIA NIVOSA ROSEOPICTA
Leaf Flower

You will find **B.nivosa** in more garden centres than textbooks. The oval leaves are 1 in. across — green, marbled with white. The variety **roseopicta** is the usual choice. The pink, white and green variegated leaves have a flower-like appearance — hence the common name.

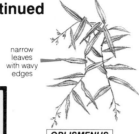

narrow leaves with wavy edges

OPLISMENUS HIRTELLUS
Basket Grass

The one you are most likely to see is **Oplismenus hirtellus variegatus (Panicum variegatum)**. Its 3–4 in. leaves on branching stems are gaily striped with white and pink. An attractive alternative to Tradescantia, but it loses its charm with age. Take new cuttings each year.

Oplismenus hirtellus variegatus

Pellaea rotundifolia

round, leathery leaflets on low-growing fronds

PELLAEA ROTUNDIFOLIA
Button Fern

A true fern, despite its appearance. The foot-long arching fronds arise from a creeping root-stock, and along the brown wiry stalk the pairs of shiny leaflets appear. These ½ in. leaflets are round at first — later oval.

oval, green leaf with pale central area

PELLIONIA DAVEAUANA

There are two Pellionias. The one above (Watermelon Pellionia) bears a pale central band on each leaf — the outer margin may be olive or bronzy-green. The photograph shows the Satin Pellionia — look for the very dark veins on the upper surface and purple colour below.

Pellionia pulchra

leaf 2 in. long

green, broadly edged with yellow

waxy surface

pink leaf stalks and stems

PEPEROMIA SCANDENS VARIEGATA
Cupid Peperomia

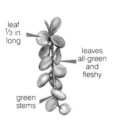

leaf ⅓ in. long

leaves all-green and fleshy

green stems

PEPEROMIA ROTUNDIFOLIA

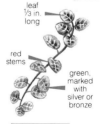

leaf ⅓ in. long

red stems

green, marked with silver or bronze

PEPEROMIA PROSTRATA
Creeping Peperomia

Peperomia scandens variegata

The bushy Peperomias are much better known than the trailing ones, although the brightly-coloured Cupid Peperomia has become quite popular. Its stems grow about 3 ft long, and this plant can be used as either a climber or trailer. The other Peperomia trailers are not widely available. Both **P. prostrata** and **P. rotundifolia** have tiny round leaves, and the experts argue about their identification. **P. glabella variegata** is easily recognised by its white-edged leaves, but it's not easy to find a supplier.

Pilea nummulariifolia

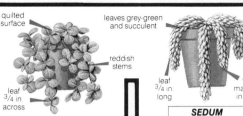

quilted surface

reddish stems

leaf ¾ in. across

PILEA NUMMULARIIFOLIA
Creeping Charlie

Turn to the bushy Pileas (page 54) if you want a colourful plant — all you will find here are two plain trailers. Apart from **P. nummulariifolia** shown above, there is **P. depressa** (Creeping Jenny). The fleshy green leaves are ¼ in. across.

leaves grey-green and succulent

leaf ¾ in. long

pink flowers may appear in summer

SEDUM MORGANIANUM
Donkey's Tail

The two trailing Sedums do not look like sisters. **S. morganianum** bears 2–3 ft long stems, completely clothed with cylindrical leaves. The thin stems of **S. sieboldii mediovariegatum** bear leaves in clusters of three. Each ¾ in. leaf is cream-hearted and edged blue-green.

Sedum sieboldii mediovariegatum

Selaginella kraussiana aurea

leaves blue-green

straw-coloured stems

leaf ⅛ in. long

SELAGINELLA UNCINATA

Selaginellas include **S. uncinata** (illustrated above), **S. apoda** (pale green, mossy) and **S. kraussiana aurea** (yellow, mat-like). **S. lepidophylla** is the Resurrection Plant which is bought dry and turns green and ferny in water.

leaves green and spherical

thread-like stems

leaf ¼ in. across

SENECIO ROWLEYANUS
String of Beads

This group of Senecios is strange indeed — pendent threads bearing bead-like leaves. **S. rowleyanus** (pea-like foliage) **S. herreianus** (oval foliage) **S. citriformis** (lemon-shaped foliage).

Senecio herreianus

Setcreasea purpurea

leaves and stems purple

leaf 5 in. long

SETCREASEA PURPUREA
Purple Heart

A straggly plant which makes up for its untidiness by its attractive colour — a rich purple when grown in good light. The leaves are slightly hairy and pink flowers appear in summer.

green, banded with creamy-white

leaf 5 in. long

STENOTAPHRUM SECUNDATUM VARIEGATUM
Buffalo Grass
(St. Augustine's Grass)

The distinctive feature is the uniform width of the foliage along its whole length. The flattened stems creep for a foot or more, adding colour to plain green arrangements.

Stenotaphrum secundatum variegatum

● OTHER CLIMBERS AND TRAILERS continued

Mikania ternata

leaf 2 in. long

underside purple

MIKANIA TERNATA
Plush Vine

A quick-growing trailing plant which has entered the shops but not the textbooks. The palmate leaves are green with a purplish sheen, slightly hairy above and densely below. An interesting new one to try as a change from ivy.

leaf 1½ in. long

yellowish-green edge

COLEUS PUMILUS TRAILING QUEEN
Trailing Coleus

Coleus is usually bought as an upright bush — one of the scores of C. blumei varieties which are available. There is however a trailing species — **C. pumilus**, sometimes listed as **C. rehneltianus**. Several varieties are sold — you can obtain seed of one or two such as **Scarlet Poncho**.

Coleus Scarlet Poncho

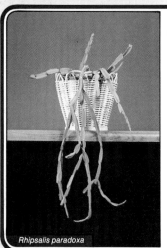

Rhipsalis paradoxa

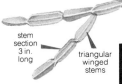

stem section 3 in. long

triangular winged stems

RHIPSALIS PARADOXA
Chain Cactus

The stems of **Rhipsalis paradoxa** are narrowed at intervals, giving a branched chain effect. Several other pendent Rhipsalis species are grown — the summer flowers are usually of little interest but one species (**R. cassutha**) is grown for its berries — see page 71.

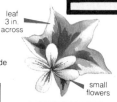

stem 3–6 ft long

slender, branching stems

BOWIEA VOLUBILIS
Climbing Onion

The Climbing Onion is grown as a thing of curiosity rather than beauty. The large above-ground bulb produces thin and straggly stems in autumn. A few short-lived leaves and small greenish flowers appear before the stems die down in late spring.

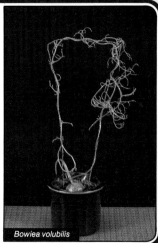

Bowiea volubilis

Begonia solanthera

leaf 4 in. across

underside red

BEGONIA IMPERIALIS
Carpet Begonia

Basket Begonias are grown for their floral display (see page 75) but a few trailing and creeping foliage Begonias are occasionally seen. Examples are **Begonia solanthera** (waxy foliage) and **B. imperialis** (velvety foliage). **B. foliosa** bears tiny oval leaves and pendent stems, giving a fern-like effect.

leaf 3 in. across

small flowers

PELARGONIUM PELTATUM L'ELEGANTE
Ivy-leaved Geranium

The Ivy-leaved or Trailing Geranium (**Pelargonium peltatum**) is a popular hanging-basket plant. Grown primarily for its flowers (see page 75), there are a few varieties which bear decorative foliage. The white-edged **L'Elégante** is an example — so is the creamy-veined **Sussex Lace**.

Pelargonium peltatum Sussex Lace

Grassy-leaved Plants

Apart from Chlorophytum (page 24) and Cyperus (page 11), very few grass-like varieties are grown as house plants. Long and narrow leaves appear to be generally unacceptable for indoor use, and yet they provide an excellent contrast to large-leaved specimens in a mixed arrangement. The ones which are available are shown on this page . . . and not one of them belongs to the Grass family.

Acorus gramineus variegatus

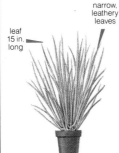

narrow, leathery leaves

leaf 15 in. long

ACORUS GRAMINEUS
Sweet Flag

Acorus grows in clumps, the leaves spreading out like a fan. Not showy, but useful in a bottle garden. Moisture-loving, so keep the soil damp at all times. The one to buy is the white-striped **A. gramineus variegatus**.

arching leaves

leaf 1 ft long

CAREX MORROWII VARIEGATA
Japanese Sedge

The grass-like leaves bear a broad creamy-white stripe. It has a cast-iron constitution and the foliage is much narrower than the leaves of Chlorophytum. An excellent choice for a small mixed bowl or trough — but hardly anyone sells it.

Carex morrowii variegata

Ophiopogon jaburan variegata

leaf 8 in. long

blackish-green leaves

OPHIOPOGON JAPONICUS
Dwarf Lily Turf

Ophiopogon japonicus is the Dwarf Lily Turf, bearing short leaves and insignificant flowers. **O. jaburan** or White Lily Turf is taller (2ft) and the clusters of white flowers in summer are more prominent. Do not confuse with Liriope (page 85).

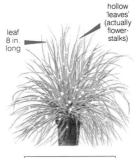

leaf 8 in. long

hollow 'leaves' (actually flower-stalks)

SCIRPUS CERNUUS
(*ISOLEPIS GRACILIS*)
Miniature Bulrush

The glossy thread-like 'leaves' are at first upright but later arch downwards. A tiny white flower appears at the tip of each leaf-like stalk. This is a plant for a hanging basket or the front of a trough, but it is hard to find a supplier.

Scirpus cernuus

Baby-bearing Plants

Many low-growing succulents form daughter plants (offsets) around the base of their stems. There are several other house plants, both succulent and non-succulent, which produce daughter plants either at the ends of long runners or on their leaves. These plantlets can be used for propagation as they root readily, and the plants with baby-bearing runners are widely used in hanging baskets and on pedestals.

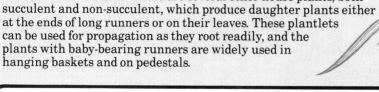

● PLANTLETS ON RUNNERS

green, edged with white and pink

leaf 1½ in. across

underside red

green, banded with creamy-white

leaf 9 in. long

SAXIFRAGA SARMENTOSA TRICOLOR

Mother of Thousands
(Magic Carpet)

CHLOROPHYTUM COMOSUM VITTATUM

Spider Plant
(St. Bernard's Lily)

Saxifraga sarmentosa

Chlorophytum comosum vittatum

Saxifraga sarmentosa (S.stolonifera) bears silver-veined olive green leaves, and is more vigorous and larger than its colourful variety **tricolor** shown above. The somewhat bristly plants grow about 9 in. high, and the pendent runners can reach 2–3 ft.

One of the most popular of all foliage house plants. Arching leaves form an attractive rosette, and in summer long stalks appear, bearing white flowers at first and then plantlets. Several varieties are available. **Vittatum** is the usual one — **variegatum** has green leaves edged with white.

● PLANTLETS ON LEAVES

frond 2 ft long

feathery fronds

dark wiry stalks

cylindrical leaf with furrow along upper surface

leaf 3 in. long

green, blotched with brown

leaf 4 in. long

fleshy, shiny leaves

underside blotched with purple

leaf 2 in. across

leaf stalk 4 in. long

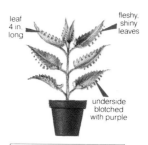

ASPLENIUM BULBIFERUM

Mother Fern

BRYOPHYLLUM TUBIFLORUM
(KALANCHOE TUBIFLORA)

Chandelier Plant

BRYOPHYLLUM DAIGREMONTIANUM
(KALANCHOE DAIGREMONTIANUM)

Devil's Backbone

TOLMIEA MENZIESII

Piggyback Plant

The fronds of the Mother or Hen-and-Chicken Fern are finely divided, and when mature bear numerous tiny plantlets known as bulbils. **Asplenium viviparum** is smaller and the fronds are more arching with stalks which are green rather than brown.

A series of tubular leaves encircle the stem, and at the tip of each fleshy leaf a small group of plantlets appear. It is an imposing plant, standing about 3 ft high, and in early spring a crown of bell-shaped orange flowers appears at the top of the stem.

An upright, unbranched succulent growing up to 2–3 ft tall. The triangular leaves, held stiffly at an angle on the stem, are curled inwards at the edges. These edges are serrated, and between the teeth tiny plantlets appear.

Tolmiea menziesii is the most popular of the types which bear plantlets on their leaves — it is easy to grow even in poor conditions where little else will survive. A 9 in. mound of downy green foliage is formed, and at the base of mature leaves the small plantlets appear. The long leaf stalks give the plant a trailing appearance.

Herringbone Plants

Two important groups of plants, the palms and the ferns, have leaves (fronds) in which the leaflets are usually arranged in a herringbone pattern. The palms are dealt with on pages 8–10; the fronds are generally large and the veins run along and not across the leaflets. In this section the rest of the herringbone plants are described, and most of them are ferns.

Not all the house plant ferns are to be found here — there are examples in several other sections — Climbers & Trailers, Upright Plants, Baby-bearing Plants, Spear-leaved Plants, etc. Nor is this particular foliage pattern restricted to the fern family — in this section you will find unrelated plants such as Jacaranda, Asparagus Fern and the Silk Oak.

There are two general patterns — the single herringbone (pinnate or pinnatifid in technical language) and the double herringbone (bipinnatifid).

● BROKEN HERRINGBONE

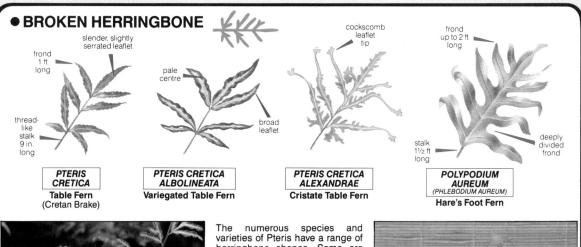

frond 1 ft long
slender, slightly serrated leaflet
thread-like stalk 9 in. long

PTERIS CRETICA
Table Fern
(Cretan Brake)

pale centre
broad leaflet

PTERIS CRETICA ALBOLINEATA
Variegated Table Fern

cockscomb leaflet tip

PTERIS CRETICA ALEXANDRAE
Cristate Table Fern

frond up to 2 ft long
stalk 1½ ft long
deeply divided frond

POLYPODIUM AUREUM
(PHLEBODIUM AUREUM)
Hare's Foot Fern

Pteris ensiformis victoriae

The numerous species and varieties of Pteris have a range of herringbone shapes. Some are neat single- or double-herringbone patterns, but an important group have irregularly-arranged fronds — the broken herringbones. The varieties of **Pteris cretica** have an assortment of leaflet colours and shapes — all-green or variegated, plain or crested. **Wilsonii** (Fan Table Fern) grows less than a foot high and has fern-like tips. The prettiest Table Fern is **P. ensiformis victoriae** with silver bands along the midribs of the leaflets. **Polypodium aureum** is a much bigger plant with large and wavy fronds. At the base is a thick, furry rhizome which creeps along the surface — hence the common name. The most attractive variety is **mandaianum** — blue-green fronds with curly margins.

Polypodium aureum mandaianum

● SINGLE HERRINGBONE

young fronds
coppery-pink

fronds
forked
at base

**ADIANTUM
HISPIDULUM**

Australian Maidenhair
(Rose Maidenhair)

narrow
leaflets

paw-like
rhizome

broad
leaflets

**AGLAOMORPHA
MEYENIANA**

Bear's Paw Fern

large palm-like
crown of stiff fronds;
trunk develops
with age

**BLECHNUM
GIBBUM**

holly-shaped
leaflets, glossy
dark green

**CYRTOMIUM
FALCATUM**

Holly Fern
(Fishtail Fern)

leathery
brownish-
green
fronds

**DIDYMOCHLAENA
TRUNCATULA**

Cloak Fern

upright,
pointed
fronds;
strap-like
leaflets

**POLYSTICHUM
ACROSTICHIOIDES**

Christmas Fern

Only one of the single-herringbone plants is not a fern — **Mimosa pudica.** This 2 ft branching plant is easily recognised by its habit of rapidly folding up its leaves when touched. Small ball-like flowers appear in summer. The ferns in this section are a highly varied group, ranging from popular house plants to rare conservatory types. The outstanding single-herringbone fern is Nephrolepis, the Sword Fern. The two basic species (**Nephrolepis cordifolia** with its 2 ft fronds and the larger **N. exaltata**) produce stiff and erect foliage, and have lost their Victorian popularity. Nearly 100 years ago a gracefully drooping variety was discovered in Boston. This was named **N. exaltata bostoniensis**, and it has become very popular on both sides of the Atlantic. There are scores of different types — some have a single-herringbone leaflet pattern — examples are **rooseveltii** (full with wavy leaflets), **maassii** (compact with wavy leaflets) and **scottii** (compact with rolled leaflets).

Less popular than the Boston Ferns but still readily available are the Holly Fern (buy the variety **rochfordianum** if you can) and the palm-like Blechnums. The usual variety is **Blechnum gibbum,** but you might find the Brazilian Tree Fern **B. braziliense**. In both cases a 3 ft trunk develops with age. The remaining ferns are not often seen as house plants. The well-known outdoor Wall Fern finds little favour indoors. The rarely-seen Bear's Paw Fern is unusual — the leaflets at the base of the fronds are much wider than the thread-like terminal ones, and the creeping rhizome is large and furry.

plain
leaf
edges

erect
fronds

**NEPHROLEPIS
EXALTATA**

Sword Fern

graceful,
arching
fronds

**NEPHROLEPIS EXALTATA
BOSTONIENSIS**

Boston Fern

leaves fold
when touched

**MIMOSA
PUDICA**

Sensitive Plant

leaflets
smooth or
slightly
toothed

**POLYPODIUM
VULGARE**

Wall Fern

glossy
leaflets:
less
leathery
than
Holly
Fern

**PELLAEA VIRIDIS
MACROPHYLLA**

arching
fronds:
narrow,
widely-spaced
leaflets

**PTERIS
VITTATA**

Ladder Fern

Adiantum caudatum

Blechnum braziliense

Didymochlaena truncatula

Nephrolepis cordifolia

Cyrtomium falcatum

Mimosa pudica

Nephrolepis exaltata bostoniensis

Pellaea viridis macrophylla

Pteris vittata

●DOUBLE HERRINGBONE

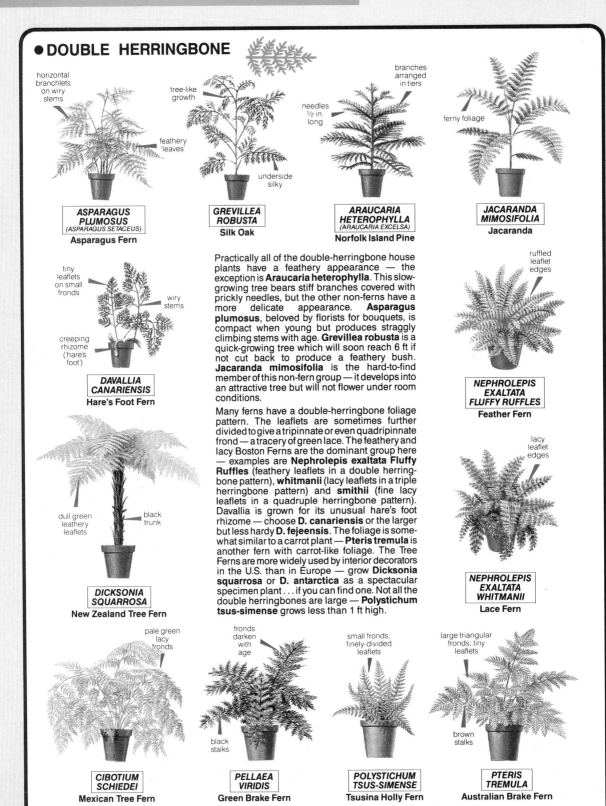

horizontal branchlets on wiry stems

feathery 'leaves'

ASPARAGUS PLUMOSUS
(ASPARAGUS SETACEUS)
Asparagus Fern

tree-like growth

underside silky

GREVILLEA ROBUSTA
Silk Oak

branches arranged in tiers

needles ½ in. long

ARAUCARIA HETEROPHYLLA
(ARAUCARIA EXCELSA)
Norfolk Island Pine

ferny foliage

JACARANDA MIMOSIFOLIA
Jacaranda

tiny leaflets on small fronds

wiry stems

creeping rhizome ('hare's foot')

DAVALLIA CANARIENSIS
Hare's Foot Fern

Practically all of the double-herringbone house plants have a feathery appearance — the exception is **Araucaria heterophylla**. This slow-growing tree bears stiff branches covered with prickly needles, but the other non-ferns have a more delicate appearance. **Asparagus plumosus**, beloved by florists for bouquets, is compact when young but produces straggly climbing stems with age. **Grevillea robusta** is a quick-growing tree which will soon reach 6 ft if not cut back to produce a feathery bush. **Jacaranda mimosifolia** is the hard-to-find member of this non-fern group — it develops into an attractive tree but will not flower under room conditions.

Many ferns have a double-herringbone foliage pattern. The leaflets are sometimes further divided to give a tripinnate or even quadripinnate frond — a tracery of green lace. The feathery and lacy Boston Ferns are the dominant group here — examples are **Nephrolepis exaltata Fluffy Ruffles** (feathery leaflets in a double herring-bone pattern), **whitmanii** (lacy leaflets in a triple herringbone pattern) and **smithii** (fine lacy leaflets in a quadruple herringbone pattern). Davallia is grown for its unusual hare's foot rhizome — choose **D. canariensis** or the larger but less hardy **D. fejeensis**. The foliage is some-what similar to a carrot plant — **Pteris tremula** is another fern with carrot-like foliage. The Tree Ferns are more widely used by interior decorators in the U.S. than in Europe — grow **Dicksonia squarrosa** or **D. antarctica** as a spectacular specimen plant . . . if you can find one. Not all the double herringbones are large — **Polystichum tsus-simense** grows less than 1 ft high.

ruffled leaflet edges

NEPHROLEPIS EXALTATA FLUFFY RUFFLES
Feather Fern

lacy leaflet edges

NEPHROLEPIS EXALTATA WHITMANII
Lace Fern

dull green leathery leaflets

black trunk

DICKSONIA SQUARROSA
New Zealand Tree Fern

pale green lacy fronds

CIBOTIUM SCHIEDEI
Mexican Tree Fern

fronds darken with age

black stalks

PELLAEA VIRIDIS
Green Brake Fern

small fronds; finely-divided leaflets

POLYSTICHUM TSUS-SIMENSE
Tsusina Holly Fern

large triangular fronds; tiny leaflets

brown stalks

PTERIS TREMULA
Australian Brake Fern

Araucaria heterophylla

Asparagus plumosus

Jacaranda mimosifolia

Grevillea robusta

Nephrolepis exaltata Gloriosa

Davallia canariensis

Dicksonia antarctica

Pteris tremula

Polystichum tsus-simense

Lobed & Star-leaved Plants

There are a number of bushy foliage house plants which bear distinctly lobed leaves. These lobes may be irregular in outline or neat and symmetrical, forming a hand- or star-shaped pattern. No family ties bind the various plants in this group — several completely unrelated genera are found and the sizes range from a small begonia in a 5 in. pot to the Tree Philodendron with leaves as long as a man's arm.

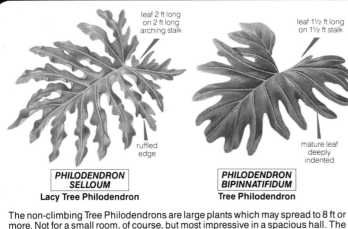

leaf 2 ft long on 2 ft long arching stalk

ruffled edge

PHILODENDRON SELLOUM
Lacy Tree Philodendron

leaf 1½ ft long on 1½ ft stalk

mature leaf deeply indented

PHILODENDRON BIPINNATIFIDUM
Tree Philodendron

Philodendron bipinnatifidum

The non-climbing Tree Philodendrons are large plants which may spread to 8 ft or more. Not for a small room, of course, but most impressive in a spacious hall. The two types are quite similar — large, deeply-cut leaves on long stalks with stems which become trunk-like with age. **Philodendron selloum** is the one seen in the U.S. — **P. bipinnatifidum** is shorter (mature height 4 ft) and is the species sold in Britain.

Platycerium bifurcatum

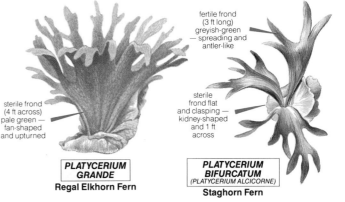

sterile frond (4 ft across) pale green — fan-shaped and upturned

fertile frond (3 ft long) greyish-green — spreading and antler-like

sterile frond flat and clasping — kidney-shaped and 1 ft across

PLATYCERIUM GRANDE
Regal Elkhorn Fern

PLATYCERIUM BIFURCATUM
(PLATYCERIUM ALCICORNE)
Staghorn Fern

The Staghorn and Elkhorn Ferns bear large and spectacular fronds, usually divided at their ends into antler-like lobes. The fronds are of two distinct types — there are sterile fronds at the base and spore-bearing fertile fronds above. **Platycerium bifurcatum** is the popular and easy-to-grow species — the fertile fronds are the showy ones. **P. grande** is larger, and here it is the sterile fronds rather than the fertile ones which provide the display.

PELARGONIUM CAPITATUM	PELARGONIUM CRISPUM	PELARGONIUM GRAVEOLENS	PELARGONIUM TOMENTOSUM
Rose Geranium	**Lemon Geranium**	**Rose Geranium**	**Mint Geranium**

It is, of course, the flowering varieties which are responsible for the popularity of the geranium, but there are several which are grown for their foliage rather than their small flowers. These are the Scented-leaved Geraniums, and the common names describe the aroma when the leaves are gently crushed. Some examples are shown here — **Pelargonium capitatum** (3 ft, pink flowers), **P. crispum** (2 ft, pink flowers), **P. graveolens** (3 ft, rose-red flowers) and **P. tomentosum** (2 ft, white flowers). There are other aromas, such as **P. fragrans** (nutmeg) and **P. Prince of Orange** (orange). Cut back occasionally to maintain bushiness.

Pelargonium crispum

Abutilon striatum thompsonii

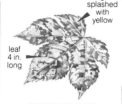

dark green, splashed with yellow

leaf 4 in. long

ABUTILON STRIATUM THOMPSONII

Spotted Flowering Maple

The Flowering Maples are generally grown for their blooms (see page 114) but this variety is best known for its variegated leaves. The orange blooms in summer are a bonus. Quickgrowing — can reach 5 ft or more.

green, splashed with chocolate brown

leaf 2 in. long

BEGONIA CLEOPATRA

Mapleleaf Begonia

Begonia Cleopatra produces small, perfumed pink flowers on long stems, but this small bushy plant (6–9 in. high) is grown for its glistening, bronzy leaves rather than its blooms. The underside of the foliage bears white hairs.

Begonia Cleopatra

Fatsia japonica

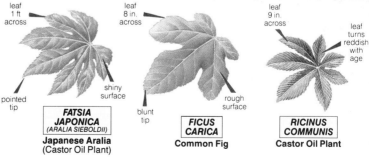

leaf 1 ft across

pointed tip

shiny surface

FATSIA JAPONICA (ARALIA SIEBOLDII)

Japanese Aralia (Castor Oil Plant)

leaf 8 in. across

blunt tip

rough surface

FICUS CARICA

Common Fig

leaf 9 in. across

leaf turns reddish with age

RICINUS COMMUNIS

Castor Oil Plant

Several plants bear leaves which are divided into finger-like lobes. Only one is popular — the old favourite **Fatsia japonica**. This shrub will grow several feet tall in a couple of years and can be kept indoors or out. There are several varieties, including **variegata** (cream-edged leaves) and **moseri** (compact growth habit). The other plants with finger-lobed leaves are much less popular — there are **Ricinus communis** (leaves more deeply divided than Fatsia foliage) and **Ficus carica** (passed over for its better-known relatives such as the Rubber Plant).

False Palms

The False Palms are an extremely important group of house plants containing some of the modest specimens found on sideboards in living rooms as well as some of the giants which grace the foyers of public buildings. At the young stage the stem is short and completely clothed by the leaf bases. This means that the palm effect is absent — the specimen looks like a typical Rosette Plant (page 36). With age the stem elongates and it is usual for the lower leaves to be lost. In this way the characteristic palm-like appearance is created — a bare stem or trunk with a crown of long leaves.

This section is dominated by the Cordylines, Dracaenas, Dieffenbachias and Yuccas. A number of other plants are also listed here, and there are several in other sections which can develop a False Palm appearance when fully grown. The Bromeliads (page 36) are the most important examples as many of them lose their flat rosette habit as they mature. An old specimen of Aglaonema (page 44) usually develops a short stem and may take on the False Palm habit of Dieffenbachia. It is, however, not included here because most examples produce several stems rather than a single trunk.

● **CORDYLINES**   The species and varieties of Cordylines are often confused with and sold as Dracaenas, but there are clear-cut differences. Cordylines have a creeping rootstock and the roots are generally white when cut. Dracaenas have a non-creeping rootstock and the roots are yellow.

Cordyline terminalis Kiwi

leaf
1 ft
long

green, splashed with red, pink and cream

CORDYLINE TERMINALIS TRICOLOR

leaf
9 in.
long

green, streaked with red

CORDYLINE TERMINALIS REDEDGE

leaf
1 ft
long

plain green

CORDYLINE TERMINALIS TI

4–6 ft high

dull, rough-edged leaves

CORDYLINE STRICTA

Cordyline terminalis (often sold as **Dracaena terminalis**) is the only popular one and has many common names — Goodluck Plant, Ti Plant, Red Dracaena, Polynesian Ti and so on. The leaves are usually tinged or splashed with red and there are many varieties of this compact 1–2 ft False Palm. **Rededge** is the favourite one — you can buy many others such as **Prince Albert** (green and red), **Fire-brand** (bronze), **amabilis** (green and white) and **baptistii** (green, pink and yellow). **Ti** is all-green and is the 'grass' used for hula skirts in Hawaii — most all-green varieties are not suitable for ordinary room conditions but **volckaertii** is a tolerant exception. New varieties of C. terminalis continue to appear — look for **Atom** and **Kiwi**.

3–4 ft high

long, narrow and arching leaves

CORDYLINE AUSTRALIS
(DRACAENA INDIVISA)
Cabbage Tree
(Grass Palm)

● DRACAENAS

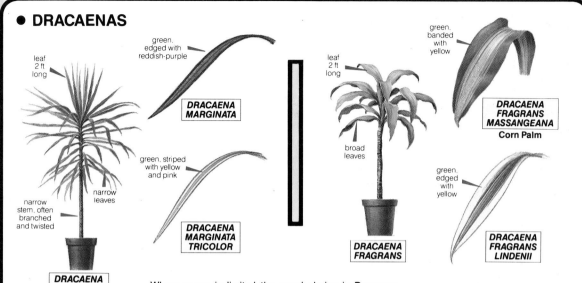

leaf 2 ft long

green, edged with reddish-purple

DRACAENA MARGINATA

narrow leaves

green, striped with yellow and pink

narrow stem, often branched and twisted

DRACAENA MARGINATA TRICOLOR

DRACAENA MARGINATA
Madagascar Dragon Tree

leaf 2 ft long

broad leaves

green, banded with yellow

DRACAENA FRAGRANS MASSANGEANA
Corn Palm

DRACAENA FRAGRANS

green, edged with yellow

DRACAENA FRAGRANS LINDENII

leaf 9 in. long

green, edged with white

DRACAENA SANDERANA
Ribbon Plant

Where space is limited the usual choice is **Dracaena sanderana**. The twisted leaves are not wide spreading and the maximum height is no more than 2–3 ft. **D. marginata** is quite different — its branching snake-like trunk can grow up to 10 ft high and with its crown of shiny narrow leaves is much loved by interior decorators. The variety **tricolor** is more colourful and is an established favourite — **colorama** is a more recent introduction and is quite widely available. **D. fragrans** is a much more solid plant and is often grown as a Ti Tree (page 35). On top of the stout trunk there is a crown of glossy leaves which are about 4 in. wide. Several varieties such as **Victoria** (broad yellow stripe) are available but **massangeana** outsells all the others. **D. draco** is a giant in its natural habitat but grows to only 4 ft in the home. The bluish leaves are red-edged if kept in good light. **D. deremensis** has many varieties but only a few are widely available — you should be able to find the species and its varieties **warneckii** and the diminutive **compacta**. The tall-growing **D. hookeriana** (narrow green leaves edged with white) is listed in some books but is rarely seen for sale.

leaf 1½ ft long

tough, sword-shaped leaves — resin ('dragon's blood') exudes from trunk

DRACAENA DRACO
Dragon Tree

Dracaena marginata tricolor

Dracaena fragrans massangeana

Dracaena sanderana

● DRACAENAS continued

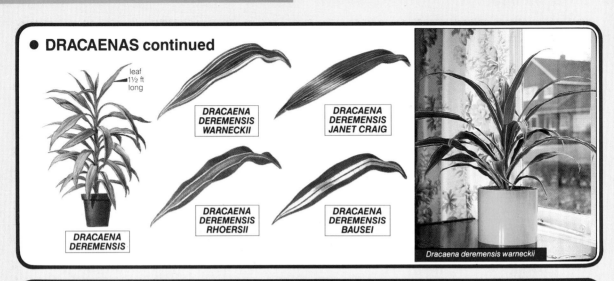

leaf 1½ ft long

DRACAENA DEREMENSIS WARNECKII

DRACAENA DEREMENSIS JANET CRAIG

DRACAENA DEREMENSIS RHOERSII

DRACAENA DEREMENSIS BAUSEI

DRACAENA DEREMENSIS

Dracaena deremensis warneckii

● DIEFFENBACHIAS

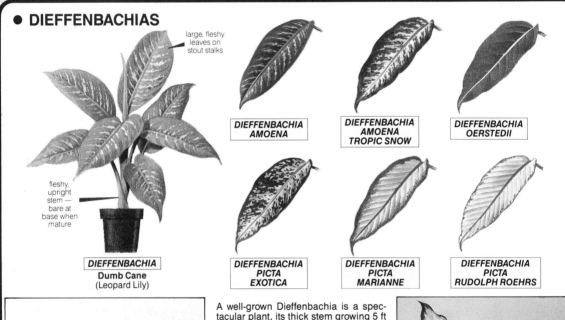

large, fleshy leaves on stout stalks

fleshy, upright stem — bare at base when mature

DIEFFENBACHIA
Dumb Cane
(Leopard Lily)

DIEFFENBACHIA AMOENA

DIEFFENBACHIA AMOENA TROPIC SNOW

DIEFFENBACHIA OERSTEDII

DIEFFENBACHIA PICTA EXOTICA

DIEFFENBACHIA PICTA MARIANNE

DIEFFENBACHIA PICTA RUDOLPH ROEHRS

Dieffenbachia amoena Tropic Snow

A well-grown Dieffenbachia is a spectacular plant, its thick stem growing 5 ft high with foot-long intricately-patterned leaves borne along its length. Its common name (Dumb Cane) is derived from the unpleasant effect of its poisonous sap on the mouth and throat. One of the largest species is **Dieffenbachia amoena** with leaves up to 18 in. long. The dark green leaves are striped with white bars — the effect is most striking in the variety **Tropic Snow**. The most popular species is **D. picta**, sometimes sold as **D. maculata**. The leaves are about 10 in. long, and they range from nearly all-green to practically all-cream. **Exotica** is heavily splashed with ivory — **Marianne** is even paler. For a compact plant, choose **compacta** or **Camilla**. All-green Dieffenbachias are hard to find — there are **D. humilis** and **D. oerstedii** . . . if you can locate a supplier.

Dieffenbachia picta Camilla

● OTHER FALSE PALMS

Pleomele reflexa variegata

leaf 6 in. long

green, edged with yellow

PLEOMELE REFLEXA VARIEGATA
Song of India

Slow-growing and colourful, this False Palm is compact enough for a small room. The only Pleomele you are likely to find is Song of India — the slender stem will require staking once the lower leaves have fallen.

leaf 2–3 ft long

saw-edged leaves

leaves spirally arranged on stem

PANDANUS VEITCHII
Screw Pine

Pandanus veitchii is wide-spreading and reaches a height of about 4 ft. The serrated leaf edges are sharp — grow the variety **compacta** to keep the foliage out of harm's way. **P. baptistii** has smooth-edged leaves.

Pandanus veitchii

Yucca elephantipes

leaf 3 ft long

rough-edged leaves

swollen base

YUCCA ELEPHANTIPES
Spineless Yucca

The 3-5 ft woody trunk bears a crown of long, leathery leaves. Choose **Y. elephantipes** — safer than **Y. aloifolia** (Spanish Bayonet) with sword-like leaves.

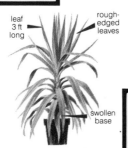

leaf 3-5 ft long

swollen base

BEAUCARNEA RECURVATA
(NOLINA TUBERCULATA)
Pony Tail
(Elephant Foot)

A shaggy-looking False Palm which is a talking point. It grows slowly, but with time the trunk will grow to 6 ft or more and the base will be swollen like a huge bulb.

Beaucarnea recurvata

The Ti Tree

Ti Trees are grown by planting pieces of mature cane cut from Dracaena, Cordyline or Yucca. The crown of leaves which appears at the top of the cane after planting provides an 'instant palm' effect. Nursery-raised Ti Trees can be bought from garden centres and other outlets, but you can grow your own. Ti Canes, cut from outdoor tropical plants and dried before shipment are now widely available in both garden and gift shops.

leaf 1 ft long

boat-shaped bracts containing tiny flowers

underside purple

RHOEO DISCOLOR
Boat Lily

The trunk is short and the leaves are glossy and fleshy. Small white flowers in purple 'boats' are responsible for one of the common names — Moses in the Cradle.

Rhoeo discolor vittata

Rosette Plants

A Rosette Plant bears leaves which radiate symmetrically from a central point, and each ring of leaves overlaps the one below. No distinct stem is visible and the rosette is usually low growing.

Many foliage house plants exhibit this growth pattern but they virtually all belong to just two groups — the Bromeliads and the Succulent Rosettes. Without a tight rosette neither would survive in its natural habitat. For Bromeliads the rosette produces a central 'vase' to hold water in the jungle — for Succulent Rosettes it is a way of tightly packing the leaves and so cutting down water loss in the desert.

In both cases the standard rosette pattern may change with age. Some Bromeliads form an elongated foliage-covered base (pseudo-trunk), whereas some succulents develop a true trunk and become rosette trees. These plants with their woody stems and leafy crowns are grouped with the Bushy & Upright Succulents (pages 46—49). These rosette trees begin life as simple Succulent Rosettes, so it may be necessary to check both sections before you can identify a plant which bears low-growing fleshy leaves.

● BROMELIADS

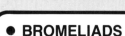

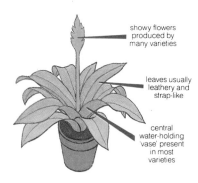

showy flowers produced by many varieties

leaves usually leathery and strap-like

central water-holding 'vase' present in most varieties

It is not surprising that interior decorators who specialise in indoor plants regard the Bromeliads as an essential part of their stock-in-trade. In this group of plants you will find brilliant foliage colour, striking flowers . . . and novelty. The vase-forming varieties shown in this section can be attached to driftwood, dead branches etc and watered by keeping the central cup topped up. On page 7 you will find Bromeliads which take this independence from the soil even further — these Air Plants do not require watering at all!

Here we deal with the rosette-forming Bromeliads which are grown for the beauty of their foliage. Cryptanthus is a low-growing example — Nidularium and Neoregelia are foliage Bromeliads which often turn glowing red at the centre of the rosette when the insignificant flowers appear.

Three Bromeliads in this section — Aechmea, Vriesea and Guzmania, are widely grown for their brightly-coloured flower-heads as well as their foliage — their flowers are shown in Chapter 5. Unfortunately the rosette starts to die as the flowers begin to open, although it may survive for a year or two. The only exception to this rule is the uncommon Dyckia, which bears rosettes which do not die after flowering.

Not all Bromeliads are foliage plants — some have little charm when not in flower. The main ones (Billbergia and Tillandsia) are dealt with in the chapter on Flowering House Plants.

saw-edged leaves

underside purple

NIDULARIUM INNOCENTII
Bird's Nest Bromeliad

Not often seen — differs from the more popular and rather similar Neoregelia by having a central rosette of very short leaves. This 'bird's nest' turns bright red at flowering time. Leaves below the bird's nest are about 1 ft long and 2 in. wide.

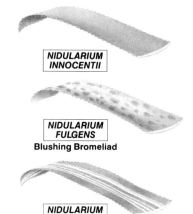

NIDULARIUM INNOCENTII

NIDULARIUM FULGENS
Blushing Bromeliad

NIDULARIUM INNOCENTII STRIATUM

Nidularium fulgens

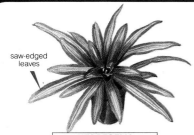

saw-edged leaves

NEOREGELIA CAROLINAE TRICOLOR
Blushing Bromeliad

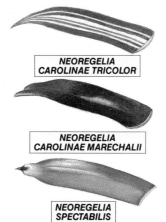

NEOREGELIA CAROLINAE TRICOLOR

NEOREGELIA CAROLINAE MARECHALII

NEOREGELIA SPECTABILIS
Fingernail Plant

Neoregelia spectabilis

The favourite variety, **Neoregelia carolinae tricolor**, blushes at the centre when about to flower, whereas the Fingernail Plant reddens at the leaf tips. The glossy leaves are about a foot long, and with age the foliage of the **tricolor** variety becomes suffused with pink.

large saw-edged leaves

AECHMEA FASCIATA
(AECHMEA RHODOCYANEA)
Urn Plant
(Vase Plant)

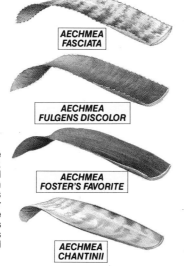

AECHMEA FASCIATA

AECHMEA FULGENS DISCOLOR

AECHMEA FOSTER'S FAVORITE

AECHMEA CHANTINII

Aechmea Foster's Favorite

The Urn Plant is good enough to be the showpiece of any living room or florist window. The arching 2 ft grey-green leaves are banded with silvery powder and the floral spike which appears when the plant is a few years old is striking (see page 101). There are other Aechmeas — **A. chantinii** is grown for its large banded leaves and bright flowers, **A. fulgens discolor** for its purple-backed foliage plus decorative berries, and where space is limited there are dwarfs like **A. Foster's Favorite**.

smooth-edged leaves

VRIESEA SPLENDENS
(VRIESEA SPECIOSA)
Flaming Sword

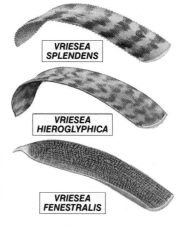

VRIESEA SPLENDENS

VRIESEA HIEROGLYPHICA

VRIESEA FENESTRALIS

Vriesea fenestralis

The usual Vriesea is **V. splendens** — dark-banded foot-long leaves and a brilliant red flower-head. There are others. **V. hieroglyphica** has interestingly-marked leaves but it rarely flowers and does not deserve its common name — King of the Bromeliads. **V. fenestralis** is also a foliage variety, grown for its finely-netted leaves rather than its blooms.

● BROMELIADS continued

CRYPTANTHUS ACAULIS
Green Earth Star

CRYPTANTHUS BIVITTATUS

CRYPTANTHUS ACAULIS ROSEO-PICTUS

CRYPTANTHUS BROMELIOIDES TRICOLOR
Rainbow Star

CRYPTANTHUS FOSTERIANUS

CRYPTANTHUS ZONATUS

small, wavy-edged leaves

CRYPTANTHUS
Earth Star

These low-growing plants are best kept in a glass container. There is a wide range to choose from — plain, striped and banded in green, red, brown and yellow. Leaf sizes range from **Cryptanthus bivittatus** (4 in.) to **C. fosterianus** (15 in.). The brightest (and most difficult to grow) is **C. bromelioides tricolor**.

Cryptanthus fosterianus

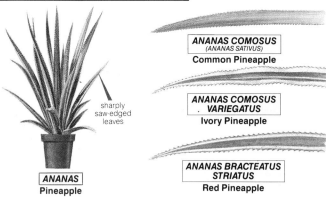

ANANAS COMOSUS
(ANANAS SATIVUS)
Common Pineapple

ANANAS COMOSUS . VARIEGATUS
Ivory Pineapple

ANANAS BRACTEATUS STRIATUS
Red Pineapple

sharply saw-edged leaves

ANANAS
Pineapple

It is possible, with care, to produce small but inedible fruits at home (see page 71) but the Pineapple Plant is generally grown for its foliage. The leaves are narrow and fiercely spined, so take care. The Common Pineapple is rather dull and too large for the living room — a much better choice is its smaller and more colourful variety **Ananas comosus variegatus**. Best of all is **A. bracteatus striatus**, bearing stiff and arching 1–2 ft leaves brightly striped with green, cream and pink.

Ananas bracteatus striatus

large, smooth-edged leaves

very wide rosette base

GUZMANIA LINGULATA
Scarlet Star

The Guzmanias are grown for their showy flower-heads as well as their leaves. **G. lingulata** (leaves 1½ ft long) is popular — the variety **minor** (pale green leaves 4 in. long) is preferred where space is limited. The most colourful foliage belongs to **G. musaica** (green banded with mahogany) but plants are usually chosen for the size and colour of their flower-heads — many hybrids are available (see page 101).

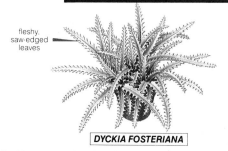

fleshy, saw-edged leaves

DYCKIA FOSTERIANA

Dyckia is certainly the least popular of the Bromeliads described in this section. Its stiff and barbed leaves are fleshy, and the rosettes have two unusual features. Daughter rosettes are freely produced so that a cluster of plants is produced with age, and the flower-heads arise from the side and not the centre of each rosette. There is the green **Dyckia brevifolia** (leaves 4 in. long) and the bronzy **D. fosteriana** (leaves 9 in. long).

● SUCCULENT ROSETTES

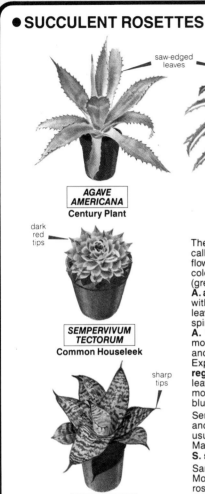

saw-edged leaves

AGAVE AMERICANA
Century Plant

fine threads

AGAVE AMERICANA MEDIOPICTA

AGAVE FILIFERA
Thread Agave

black spines at leaf tips

AGAVE VICTORIAE-REGINAE

dark red tips

SEMPERVIVUM TECTORUM
Common Houseleek

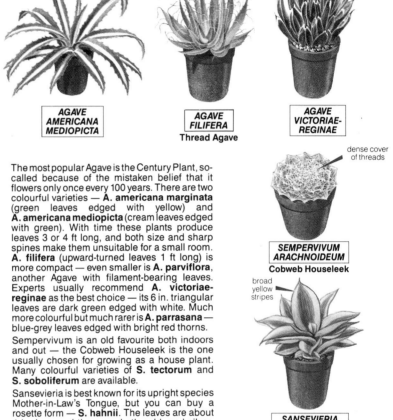

dense cover of threads

SEMPERVIVUM ARACHNOIDEUM
Cobweb Houseleek

broad yellow stripes

sharp tips

SANSEVIERIA HAHNII

SANSEVIERIA GOLDEN HAHNII
Golden Bird's Nest

The most popular Agave is the Century Plant, so-called because of the mistaken belief that it flowers only once every 100 years. There are two colourful varieties — **A. americana marginata** (green leaves edged with yellow) and **A. americana mediopicta** (cream leaves edged with green). With time these plants produce leaves 3 or 4 ft long, and both size and sharp spines make them unsuitable for a small room. **A. filifera** (upward-turned leaves 1 ft long) is more compact — even smaller is **A. parviflora**, another Agave with filament-bearing leaves. Experts usually recommend **A. victoriae-reginae** as the best choice — its 6 in. triangular leaves are dark green edged with white. Much more colourful but much rarer is **A. parrasana** — blue-grey leaves edged with bright red thorns.

Sempervivum is an old favourite both indoors and out — the Cobweb Houseleek is the one usually chosen for growing as a house plant. Many colourful varieties of **S. tectorum** and **S. soboliferum** are available.

Sansevieria is best known for its upright species Mother-in-Law's Tongue, but you can buy a rosette form — **S. hahnii**. The leaves are about 4 in. long and there are both gold- and silver-variegated versions.

Agave victoriae-reginae

Sempervivum soboliferum

Sansevieria hahnii

● SUCCULENT ROSETTES continued

white warts on leaves

ALOE ARISTATA
Lace Aloe

toothed leaves

ALOE HUMILIS
Hedgehog Aloe

white edges

thick triangular leaves

ALOE VARIEGATA
Partridge-breasted Aloe

toothed leaves

ALOE MITRIFORMIS

brown-tipped pointed leaves

ECHEVERIA AGAVOIDES

waxy leaves

ECHEVERIA GLAUCA
Blue Echeveria

flat-topped leaves

ECHEVERIA DERENBERGII
Painted Lady

red-tipped leaves

fine white hairs on leaves

ECHEVERIA SETOSA
Firecracker Plant

Aloes come in all shapes and sizes, and many form stemless rosettes of fleshy leaves. Only two of them are popular as house plants. **A. variegata** is immediately recognisable — the upright 6 in. leaves are triangular with prominent white banding and edging on the dark green or purplish surface. **A. aristata** is smaller — the 4 in. long leaves form a globular rosette which when mature readily produces a large number of offsets. There are several other attractive Aloes — **A. jacunda** is the small one, forming 3 in. rosettes of spiny, cream-blotched leaves. **A. humilis** is another dwarf, with incurving blue-green leaves. **A. mitriformis** is the thorny one.

Some Echeverias readily produce stems and grow as rosette trees — only the flattened rosette forms are described here. The short and tightly-packed leaves are covered with a white bloom, short hairs or a waxy coating. There is an exception — **E. agavoides** bears plain-surfaced, 2 in. long green leaves. Echeveria leaves are 1–3 in. long and each popular species has its own distinctive feature — the ball-like silvery rosettes of **E. elegans**, the pinkish-tinged leaves of **E. carnicolor**, the waxy, hollow-spoon leaves of **E. glauca**, the furry foliage of **E. setosa** and the red-tipped grey leaves of **E. derenbergii**.

Aloe variegata

Aloe jacunda

Echeveria elegans

white warts on leaves

HAWORTHIA MARGARITIFERA
Pearl Plant

finely-pointed leaves

HAWORTHIA FASCIATA
Zebra Haworthia

translucent upper surface

HAWORTHIA TESSELLATA
Star Window Plant

fleshy, spoon-like leaves

ADROMISCHUS COOPERI

toothed, jaw-like leaves

FAUCARIA TIGRINA
Tiger Jaws

white warts on leaves

GASTERIA VERRUCOSA
Ox Tongue

Haworthias are Aloe-like succulents which bear thick and warty leaves. **H. margaritifera** forms a ball-like rosette about 5 in. across. The white tubercles which cover the backs of the leaves give the plant a pearly appearance — **H. papillosa** is similar. The warts on **H. fasciata** are arranged in horizontal bands — this 'zebra striping' is also a feature of **H. attenuata**. Some Haworthias have semi-transparent 'windows' instead of warts on the upper leaf surface — examples are **H. tessellata** and **H. cuspidata**.

Adromischus cooperi has thick leaves with wavy tips. The grey-green foliage is splashed with purple and the reddish hairs which appear at the base are really aerial roots.

The fleshy leaves of **Faucaria tigrina** are 2 in. long 'jaws' complete with teeth. These spines are quite soft and so the plant is not as vicious as it looks.

Gasteria leaves are arranged in two rows — with age an untidy rosette is usually formed. **G. verrucosa** is the warty one — **G. maculata** has similar-sized leaves (5–6 in. long) but they are wart-free and blotched with white.

A few Succulent Rosettes are flat saucers made up of many densely-packed leaves — examples are **Aeonium tabulaeforme** and the biennial **Orostachys spinosus**.

tightly-packed waxy leaves

AEONIUM TABULAEFORME
Saucer Plant

tightly-packed pointed leaves

OROSTACHYS SPINOSUS

Haworthia attenuata

Faucaria tigrina

Gasteria maculata

Living Stones

The Living Stones are interesting rather than beautiful, as they mimic the pebbles which abound in their natural habitat. All are members of the Mesembryanthemum family and each plant consists of a pair of extremely thick leaves. These are fused together to produce a stem-like body with a slit at the top. This slit may be as small as a tiny hole or it may extend right down to ground level, depending upon the species. The sizes of the various types available do not differ very much — the range is a height of ½–2 in. Colours and patterns, however, present a bewildering array and collecting a comprehensive range of Living Stones can be a hobby in itself.

All are extremely slow growing and must be kept dry throughout the winter. Below ground there is a short stem and a long tap root — above ground white, pink or yellow daisy-like flowers appear in autumn, and after many years a clump of 'stones' will fill the pot.

Scores of different Living Stones are available. Nearly all belong to two genera — Lithops and Conophytum, and identification of individual species can be extremely difficult. In some cases leaf colour is affected by the soil type.

1 in. high, olive-green with brown markings	1½ in. high, grey-green with mottled top	1½ in. high, grey with green mottled top	1 in. high, greenish-white	1½ in. high, blue-grey	1 in. high, green with translucent top
LITHOPS PSEUDOTRUNCATELLA	**LITHOPS FULLERI**	**LITHOPS SALICOLA**	**ARGYRODERMA TESTICULARE**	**LAPIDARIA MARGARETAE**	**CONOPHYTUM FRIEDRICHAE**

The most popular Living Stones are species of Lithops. Three are illustrated above — others which are offered for sale include **L. turbiniformis** (brown, wrinkled), **L. bella** (pale brown with dark markings), **L. lesliei** (brown with green markings) and **L. optica** (grey-green with translucent 'windows' on upper surface). The cleft between the two leaves in Lithops may be shallow or deep, depending on the species, but the cleft between the leaves of Conophytum is reduced to a small fissure through which the flower stalk appears. Several species are available, including **C. bilobum** (grey-green tinged with red) and **C. calculus** (pale green).

Lithops bella

Lithops lesliei

Conophytum pearsonii nana

Insect Eaters

Some plants live in situations where their roots cannot obtain sufficient nutrients, and so they have evolved mechanisms to trap insects and then digest the contents of their bodies. There are three groups of these insectivorous plants — the **Fly Traps** with spiny-edged leaves which are hinged in the middle, the **Sticky-leaved Plants** with hairs which secrete insect-catching fluid, and the **Pitcher Plants** with leaves which are water-filled funnels. These plants are very difficult to grow indoors — water with rainwater, keep constantly moist and humid, and feed very occasionally with tiny bits of meat or dead flies.

Dionaea muscipula

Dionaea muscipula (Venus Fly Trap) is the most spectacular Insect Eater in its action but not in appearance. There is a rosette of heart-shaped leaves, each one fringed with teeth and bearing trigger hairs and red glandular hairs on the surface. When touched by an insect the 2 halves immediately close and remain closed for about 2 weeks.

Drosera capensis

Drosera (Sundew) bears a rosette of leaves covered with red glandular hairs. These hairs secrete the juices which both trap and digest the insects, and 2 species are available. **D. binata** is an Australian Sundew which bears long and deeply-lobed leaves — the American **D. capensis** has undivided leaves. Both grow 6 in. high.

Nepenthes coccinea

Nepenthes coccinea is one of the lidded Pitcher Plants — insects are attracted by the brightly-coloured pitcher. Once inside this container they drown in the pepsin solution at the base. There are other lidded Pitcher Plants — **Sarracenia drummondii** has pale green tubes streaked with purple.

Darlingtonia californica

Darlingtonia californica is a hooded Pitcher Plant. Its snake's-head appearance is responsible for the common name — Cobra Plant. The pale green pitcher will grow to 2 ft or more under ideal conditions — the heavily-veined head and dark forked tongue making this one of the strangest of plants.

Spear-leaved Plants

This small group of foliage house plants has two distinctive features. First of all, the length of their pointed non-succulent leaves is much greater than their width, giving them a distinctly spear-like appearance. Secondly there is either no stem at all or just a short one, so that the plant has a bushy rather than a tree-like appearance. Some Spear-leaved Plants, such as Aspidistras, bear leaves which grow directly out of the ground — others produce a squat, broad stem from which the leaves radiate to give a bird's nest or shuttlecock effect. The exception is Aglaonema — there are several species which occasionally produce a leafless trunk like a False Palm (see page 32) when mature.

● AGLAONEMAS

leathery leaf 8–12 in. long attached to a long stalk

short, bare stem may form when plant is mature

AGLAONEMA Chinese Evergreen

AGLAONEMA MODESTUM

AGLAONEMA COMMUTATUM SILVER SPEAR

AGLAONEMA PICTUM

AGLAONEMA SILVER QUEEN

AGLAONEMA PSEUDOBRACTEATUM

AGLAONEMA COMMUTATUM

Aglaonema Silver Queen

The Aglaonemas are popular house plants — the arum-like flowers which appear in summer are not particularly showy, so they are grown primarily for their large and colourful foliage. Aglaonemas tolerate shade, but the variegated ones are usually chosen and the need for light increases as the green area of the leaf decreases. Near-white varieties need a well-lit situation. The baby of the group is **A. pictum** (6 in. speckled and velvety leaves) — the giant is **A. nitidum** (18 in. plain green leaves). The usual plain green species is **A. modestum**, but it is the variegated types which are generally chosen. **A. commutatum** has silver bands — **A. pseudobracteatum** (Golden Evergreen) is blotched with yellow, cream and pale green. **A. commutatum Silver Spear** is an attractive variety, but perhaps the best of all the Aglaonemas are the hybrids **A. Silver Queen** and **A. Silver King** with foliage which is almost entirely silvery-grey.

Aglaonema pseudobracteatum

Aspidistra elatior variegata

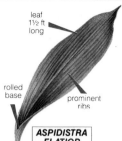

leaf 1½ ft long

rolled base

prominent ribs

ASPIDISTRA ELATIOR
Cast Iron Plant

This much-maligned symbol of the Victorian age has staged a come-back. The dark green leaves withstand both air pollution and neglect but are scorched by sunlight. A cream-striped variety (**Aspidistra elatior variegata**) is available.

leaf 1 ft long

ROHDEA JAPONICA MARGINATA
Sacred Manchu Lily

A great favourite in Japan, but hardly ever grown in Britain. The thick arching leaves of **Rohdea japonica marginata** are near-black edged with white — **R. japonica** (Lily of China) foliage is all-green. The fruit stalk grows about 1 ft tall.

Rohdea japonica

Asplenium nidus

leaf 2 ft long

brown midrib

wavy margin

ASPLENIUM NIDUS
Bird's Nest Fern

Perhaps the best of all the bird's nest plants — shiny, pale green leaves surround the fibrous nest. Not difficult, but you must not handle the young fronds.

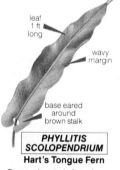

leaf 1 ft long

wavy margin

base eared around brown stalk

PHYLLITIS SCOLOPENDRIUM
Hart's Tongue Fern

Strap-shaped fronds on dark brown stalks — erect at first and then arching with age. The frond edges are wavy — the varieties **crispum** and **undulatum** have frilly margins.

Phyllitis scolopendrium undulatum

leaf 1½ ft long

wavy margin

underside purple

CALATHEA INSIGNIS
(CALATHEA LANCIFOLIA)
Rattlesnake Plant

leaf 1 ft long

underside reddish-purple

CALATHEA ZEBRINA
Zebra Plant

leaf 1½ ft long

velvety surface

velvety surface

underside reddish-purple

CTENANTHE OPPENHEIMIANA TRICOLOR
Never Never Plant

Calathea zebrina

Calatheas are highly decorative but difficult. Some have broadly oval leaves (see page 50) but there are a few species with lance-like leaves borne on long stalks. **Calathea insignis** and the smaller **C. lindeniana** bear their leaves upright — the leaves of **C. zebrina** and the smaller **C. bachemiana** are held horizontally. Ctenanthes are very similar — the one you are most likely to find is **C. oppenheimiana tricolor** with cream-coloured blotches covering a large part of the leaf surface.

Bushy & Upright Succulents

Hundreds of different succulents are cultivated as house plants, and many of them have a bushy or tree-like growth habit. Some of these Bushy & Upright Succulents are unmistakably at home in this group — the Jade Plant and Panda Plant with their fleshy leaves and upright stems could not be placed anywhere else. But borderline examples abound — does the Rat Tail Plant with its scale-like but somewhat fleshy leaves belong here or with the Bushy & Upright Plants of the non-succulent type? Echeveria harmsii is included in this section, but it grows as a Succulent Rosette (pages 39−41) for part of its life. Then there are the many Sedums which appear as small bushes in photographs but flop over the rim of the pot as trailers when grown at home.

Thus the succulents are notoriously difficult to pigeon-hole and you may have to look through the Climbers & Trailers (pages 12−22) and Succulent Rosettes (pages 39−41) sections as well as through the following few pages in order to name your plant with fleshy leaves.

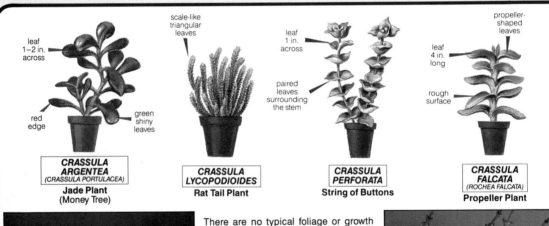

- leaf 1–2 in. across
- scale-like triangular leaves
- leaf 1 in. across
- propeller-shaped leaves
- leaf 4 in. long
- red edge
- green shiny leaves
- paired leaves surrounding the stem
- rough surface

CRASSULA ARGENTEA
(CRASSULA PORTULACEA)
Jade Plant
(Money Tree)

CRASSULA LYCOPODIOIDES
Rat Tail Plant

CRASSULA PERFORATA
String of Buttons

CRASSULA FALCATA
(ROCHEA FALCATA)
Propeller Plant

Crassula arborescens Humboldt's Sunset

There are no typical foliage or growth characteristics to help you identify a plant as a Crassula. Leaves range from scale-like to several inches long, growth habit from sprawling to stiffly erect and leaf colour from grey to red. One of the most popular species is **Crassula argentea** with its tree-like trunk growing 3 ft or more. **C. arborescens** is rather similar, but the leaves are less rounded and are greyish in colour. There are several Crassulas with stems which seem to grow through the fused leaves — **C. perforata** (2 ft tall) and the very similar **C. rupestris** are the usual ones. **C. falcata** has larger leaves than any other common Crassula — this grey-leaved, red-flowering species is easy to grow. It reaches 2–3 ft — much taller than the upright branching stems of **C. lycopodioides** which are completely clothed with minute fleshy scales. A specialist supplier will offer many others, such as **C. tetragona**, **C. turrita** and **C. dubia**.

Crassula rupestris

pinky-
bronze
leaves

**ECHEVERIA
GIBBIFLORA
METALLICA**

surface
covered
with
fine
hairs

**ECHEVERIA
HARMSII**
(OLIVERANTHUS ELEGANS)
Red Echeveria

grey-
green
leaves

**GRAPTOPETALUM
PARAGUAYENSE**
Ghost Plant

zig-
zag
stems

**PEDILANTHUS
TITHYMALOIDES**
Jacob's Ladder

saw-
edged
leaves

**ALOE
ARBORESCENS**
Tree Aloe

grey-
green
stems

**KLEINIA
ARTICULATA**
(SENECIO ARTICULATUS)
Candle Plant

There are 2 popular Echeverias which grow as rosette-topped trees. The red-tipped leaves of **E. harmsii** form a loose rosette above the branching stems. The stout trunk of **E. gibbiflora** is taller (2 ft or more) and the leaves are larger (4–6 in. long) — varieties include **crispata** (wavy edged) and **metallica** (bronzy lustre). The Graptopetalums are grey-leaved, low-growing relatives of Echeveria. **G. paraguayense** has 2 in. long leaves on 3 in. stems. **G. pachyphyllum** is a miniature tree with 1 in. high stems — the rosettes are about 1 in. across.

Pedilanthus tithymaloides is unmistakable — the fleshy stems zig-zag sharply, reaching about 2 ft. The variety **variegatus** is the popular one — oval, waxy leaves are edged with white and pink. The milky sap is an irritant, so take care.

Aloes are usually stemless rosettes but there are a few stemmed forms, including **A. arborescens** (9 in. spiny leaves on tall trunks) and **A. ferox** (18 in. spiny and warty leaves). Both species are unsuitable for small rooms.

Kleinia articulata is grown for its 2 ft bloom-coated stems. Even more dramatic is the Cocoon Plant (**K. tomentosa**) with its dense cover of white wool.

Echeveria gibbiflora carunculata

Graptopetalum pachyphyllum Rose

Aloe ferox

● BUSHY & UPRIGHT SUCCULENTS continued

leaf
1 in.
long

silvery-
white
bloom

**PACHYPHYTUM
OVIFERUM**
Sugar Almond Plant
(Moonstones)

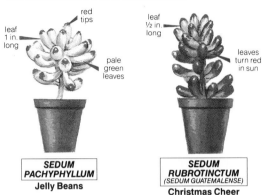

leaf
1 in.
long

red
tips

pale
green
leaves

**SEDUM
PACHYPHYLLUM**
Jelly Beans

leaf
½ in.
long

leaves
turn red
in sun

**SEDUM
RUBROTINCTUM**
(SEDUM GUATEMALENSE)
Christmas Cheer

leaf
1 in.
long

boat-
shaped
waxy
leaves

**SEDUM
ADOLPHI**
Golden Sedum

leafless
stems

milky
sap

**EUPHORBIA
TIRUCALLI**
Milk Bush
(Pencil Euphorbia)

Sedums are generally low growing with branching stems and an abundance of fleshy leaves which are either cylindrical or boat-shaped. There are, of course, exceptions — **Sedum praealtum** is a vigorous 2 ft shrub with shiny 3 in. long leaves. **S. pachyphyllum** is a typical and popular Sedum — the erect, branching stems grow about 1 ft tall and the succulent leaves are cylindrical. The tips are red and so it is easily distinguished from **S. allantoides** (leaves all-green and coated with a greyish bloom) and the compact **S. rubrotinctum** (leaves suffused with red in strong light). Species with boat-shaped leaves include **S. adolphi** and **S. bellum**.

Pachyphytum is closely related to Echeveria (see page 47). You can see the family likeness in the mauve-tinged **P. amethystinum** but the popular one is quite different — **P. oviferum** bears rosettes of egg-like leaves.

Euphorbias come in many shapes and forms, and are scattered throughout this book. Some are cactus-like (see page 62) — the thornless succulent ones include the globular **E. obesa** (Turkish Temple) and the pencil-stemmed **E. tirucalli**.

Aeonium arboreum atropurpureum has purple-leaved rosettes on top of branching stems — a mature plant can reach 3 ft or more. The variety **Schwarzkopf** has near-black foliage.

rosette
of shiny
leaves

**AEONIUM
ARBOREUM
ATROPURPUREUM**

Sedum rubrotinctum

Euphorbia obesa

Aeonium arboreum atropurpureum Schwarzkopf

SANSEVIERIA TRIFASCIATA LAURENTII

Mother-in-Law's Tongue

golden-edged leaves

sword-like foliage

SANSEVIERIA TRIFASCIATA

Snake Plant

silvery surface

wavy-edged leaves

COTYLEDON UNDULATA

Silver Crown

white warts on leaves

HAWORTHIA REINWARDTII

Wart Plant

brown-edged leaves

furry surface

KALANCHOE TOMENTOSA

Panda Plant

velvety leaves covered with brown hairs

KALANCHOE BEHARENSIS

Velvet Leaf

Sansevierias are one of the most popular of all house plants, due to the universal appeal of **S. trifasciata laurentii**. It is seen everywhere — the golden-edged and dark-banded leaves reaching 3 ft or more. The basic species **S. trifasciata** (sometimes wrongly sold as **S. zeylanica**) is smaller, plainer and much less popular, but there are other colourful varieties in addition to the overworked Mother-in-Law's Tongue. **Moonshine** is small and finely modelled in light and dark green, **Bantel's Sensation** is cross-banded with cream and **craigii** is broadly-edged with cream. The tall one (5 ft) is **S. cylindrica**.

There are many Kalanchoe varieties which are grown for their long-lasting flowers and a few which are cultivated for their striking leaves. **K. tomentosa** is perhaps the most popular of the foliage ones — 1½ ft tall with woolly leaves. There is also **K. marmorata** (Pen Wiper) with scalloped and brown-blotched leaves, and **K. beharensis** grown for its large velvety foliage.

Haworthias are generally low-growing rosettes (see page 41) but **H. reinwardtii** forms an erect 8 in. stem which is completely clothed with thick triangular leaves.

The best known Cotyledon is **C. undulata** — wavy-topped and bloom-covered leaves on 1–2 ft stems. **C. orbiculata** bears red-edged leaves.

Sansevieria trifasciata laurentii

Cotyledon orbiculata

Kalanchoe tomentosa

Bushy Plants

Bushy Plants bear plain or colourful leaves
on a number of stems which arise at or near
ground level — a single main trunk is absent.
Apart from this basic feature there are no
other common characteristics. Family ties do
not exist and the leaves vary from the small
needles of Asparagus meyeri to the 2 ft
arrowheads of Anthurium crystallinum. Some of
the plants, such as Peperomia, are short and
compact whereas others are large and shrubby —
Aucuba and Euonymus can grow several feet tall.

Some bushes have a distinctive leaf shape and have been dealt with on
previous pages. In this section the remainder are described and illustrated.

● MARANTAS

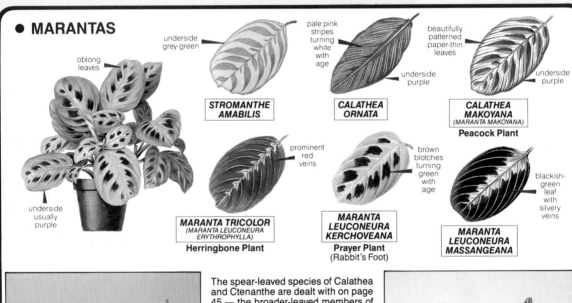

oblong
leaves

underside
grey-green

**STROMANTHE
AMABILIS**

pale pink
stripes
turning
white
with
age

underside
purple

**CALATHEA
ORNATA**

beautifully
patterned
paper-thin
leaves

underside
purple

**CALATHEA
MAKOYANA**
(MARANTA MAKOYANA)

Peacock Plant

underside
usually
purple

prominent
red
veins

MARANTA TRICOLOR
(MARANTA LEUCONEURA
ERYTHROPHYLLA)

Herringbone Plant

brown
blotches
turning
green
with
age

**MARANTA
LEUCONEURA
KERCHOVEANA**

Prayer Plant
(Rabbit's Foot)

blackish-
green
leaf
with
silvery
veins

**MARANTA
LEUCONEURA
MASSANGEANA**

The spear-leaved species of Calathea
and Ctenanthe are dealt with on page
45 — the broader-leaved members of
the Maranta group are described here.
The showpiece is undoubtedly
Calathea makoyana with 1 ft long
papery leaves borne upright on long
stalks, its decorative tracery giving rise
to one of its common names —
Cathedral Windows. The leaves of
C. ornata are smaller — choose the
variety **roseolineata** or **sanderana**.
Much less usual are **C. picturata
argentea** (silvery grey edged with
green) and **C. louisae** (dark green with
yellowish-green centre). **Stromanthe
amabilis** is a compact plant with 6 in.
long leaves — the true Marantas are
approximately the same size.
M. bicolor (dark green blotched with
brown) is available, but all the popular
varieties belong to **M. leuconeura**.
For red veins choose the variety
erythrophylla (sold as **M. tricolor**)
or **Fascinator** — for white veins pick
massangeana and for brown-spotted
leaves the usual choice is
kerchoveana.

Maranta tricolor

Calathea makoyana

● CALADIUMS

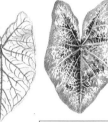

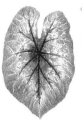

paper-thin decorative leaves

CALADIUM
Angel's Wings
(Elephant's Ears)

CALADIUM HORTULANUM CANDIDUM

CALADIUM HORTULANUM MRS HALDERMAN

CALADIUM HORTULANUM ROSEBUD

CALADIUM HORTULANUM FRIEDA HEMPLE

CALADIUM HORTULANUM LORD DERBY

Caladium hortulanum candidum

Caladium hortulanum Arno Nehrling

The colourful Caladiums are irresistible — the large arrowhead-like leaves, 1–1½ ft long, are veined, edged or splashed with a wide range of colours. The foot-long leaf-stalks arise from underground tubers. Caladiums are expensive — before buying one remember that they are difficult to grow under room conditions and the foliage dies down in winter. There are scores of varieties available but they are usually sold unnamed. The textbooks can't agree whether these hybrids should be listed under **C. bicolor** or **C. hortulanum** — obviously naming a Caladium is not easy! Several are illustrated here — **C. hortulanum candidum** is easily recognised (white with green veins) and so is its reverse image **Seagull** (green with white veins). Easier to grow than the showy hybrids is the smaller **C. humboldtii** (green blotched with white).

Anthurium crystallinum

leaf 1–2 ft long

velvety surface

ANTHURIUM CRYSTALLINUM
Crystal Anthurium

The best-known Anthurium is the Flamingo Flower (page 81) but there is a splendid foliage species — **A. crystallinum**. The leaf colour changes from bronzy-purple to deep green with age — the foliage hangs vertically, displaying the silvery veins.

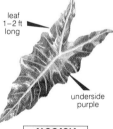

leaf 1–2 ft long

underside purple

ALOCASIA SANDERIANA
Kris Plant

Alocasias are not common, but they are worth looking for if you want a spectacular specimen plant. **A. sanderiana** has metallic green leaves with scalloped edges — **A. amazonica** is easier to find and the leaves are darker, contrasting sharply with the bold white veins.

Alocasia amazonica

Selaginella martensii watsoniana

leaf ⅛ in. long   leaves pale green

SELAGINELLA MARTENSII

Selaginellas are usually trailing plants, but **S. martensii** has upright stems which grow about 1 ft long. Aerial roots ('stilt roots') grow down from the stems into the compost — the variety **watsoniana** has silvery tips. **S. emmeliana** is another erect species, producing lacy-leaved 6 in. stems.

leaf 1 in. long   glossy, leathery leaves

BUXUS SEMPERVIRENS
Box

Box is an outdoor favourite but only recently has it moved indoors. The popular **Buxus sempervirens** can be grown, but the Small-leaved Box (**B. microphylla**) is a better choice. Slow growing — prune to keep in shape.

Buxus microphylla

Sonerila margaritacea

leaf 3 in. long   underside purple

SONERILA MARGARITACEA
Frosted Sonerila

Sonerila margaritacea is a low-growing plant with beautifully marked leaves. The surface is green or coppery green lined and spotted with silver — pink flowers appear in summer. Not easy indoors — keep it in a terrarium.

leaf 4 in. long   underside red

STENANDRIUM LINDENII

A rarity, but well worth looking for if you collect unusual plants. **Stenandrium lindenii** is a small plant bearing metallic green leaves heavily veined with bright yellow. Spikes of yellow flowers may appear.

Stenandrium lindenii

Strobilanthes dyeranus

leaf 5 in. long   underside purple

STROBILANTHES DYERANUS
Persian Shield

A lovely foliage plant when young — the leaves are dark green blotched with purple. Old plants look straggly and the colour fades from the foliage, leaving them silvery with dark veins.

'leaf' 1 in. long   dense needle-like foliage

ASPARAGUS MEYERI
Plume Asparagus
(Foxtail Fern)

A distinctive Asparagus — not ferny like the others (see page 18) but stiff and erect. The 1½ ft stems are clothed with needles (modified branchlets known as cladodes) to give a bottle-brush effect.

Asparagus meyeri

● BEGONIAS

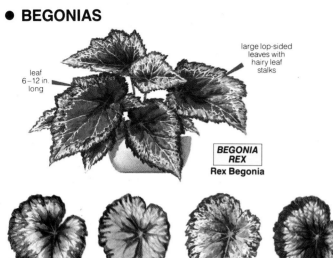

leaf 6–12 in. long

large lop-sided leaves with hairy leaf stalks

Begonia rex Bettina Rothschild

BEGONIA REX
Rex Begonia

| **BEGONIA REX MERRY CHRISTMAS** | **BEGONIA REX SILVER QUEEN** | **BEGONIA REX HER MAJESTY** | **BEGONIA REX YULETIDE** |

Many Begonias are grown for their floral display with attractive foliage as an occasional added bonus. The types described on this page are grown primarily or solely for their foliage. This group is dominated by the many hybrids of **B. rex**, so widely used in plant groups where a contrast to plain green varieties is required. Scores of varieties are available — old favourites include **President Carnot** (green and silver), **Helen Teupel** (red, green and pink) and **King Edward IV** (purple and red). Miniature Rex Begonias are available. Similar to the familiar Rex but with puckered leaves and a dark cross-shaped heart is **B. masoniana**. **B. maculata** is quite different — cane-like stems several feet high bear 9 in. long leaves, white-spotted above and red below. **B. metallica** is another tall-growing species, metallic green above and red-veined below. The Beefsteak Begonia (**B. feastii** or **B. erythrophylla**) has fleshy round leaves which are shiny green above and red below — the variety **bunchii** has leaves with crested and frilly margins. Where space is limited grow the compact **B. boweri** (6–9 in. high) or its hybrid **B. Tiger**. Most of the above Begonias and varieties produce small flowers in winter or summer, depending on the species.

Begonia feastii bunchii

purple veins

leaf 6 in. long

metallic green surface

BEGONIA METALLICA
Metallic Leaf Begonia

erect hairs

leaf 3 in. long

brown spots

BEGONIA BOWERI
Eyelash Begonia

deeply puckered leaves

leaf 6 in. long

BEGONIA MASONIANA
Iron Cross Begonia

silvery white spots

leaf 9 in. long

underside red

BEGONIA MACULATA

Begonia Tiger

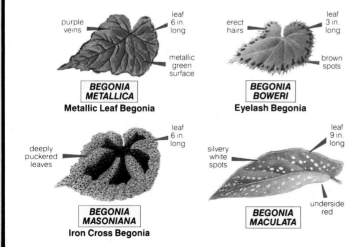

● PILEAS

leaves oval or almost round

leaf 3 in. long

silvery patches on quilted surface

PILEA CADIEREI
Aluminium Plant

leaf 2 in. long

bronzy when grown in sunlight, green when grown in shade

underside red

PILEA NORFOLK

leaf 3 in. long

dull bronzy-green, silver centre

underside red

PILEA BRONZE
(PILEA SILVER TREE)

growth habit spreading or upright

leaf 3 in. long

deeply quilted surface, vein areas brown

PILEA MOON VALLEY
(PILEA MOLLIS)

leaf 1 in. long

glossy surface, dark green or coppery

underside purple

PILEA REPENS
Black Leaf Panamiga

leaf ⅛ in. long

feathery stems with pale green leaves

PILEA MICROPHYLLA
(PILEA MUSCOSA)
Artillery Plant

Pilea Norfolk

The trailing Pileas are described on page 21 — included here are the bushy and upright ones. Almost all are grown for their decorative leaves but there is an exception — **P. microphylla** is a fern-like plant grown for the novelty of its puffs of smoke-like pollen when tapped in summer. Over the years the naming of the large-leaved Pileas has become quite confused. There is no problem with either recognising or naming the most popular species — **P. cadierei** grows about 1 ft tall and becomes leggy and unattractive with age. The variety **nana** is more compact. The species **P. spruceana** has given rise to 2 popular varieties — **P. Norfolk** and **P. Bronze**, with oval or rounded leaves in which bronze and silver dominate the quilted surface when grown in bright light. **P. involucrata**, the original Pan-American Friendship Plant is not sold as such — the popular form is **P. Moon Valley**. **P. repens** is smaller than the popular varieties, a low and spreading plant with coppery leaves.

Pilea Moon Valley

Acalypha wilkesiana

red or brown patches on leaves

leaf 5 in. long

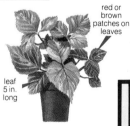

ACALYPHA WILKESIANA
Copper Leaf

A colourful shrub which can reach 4 ft or more — good light is essential to maintain the red and brown mottling. There are several fine varieties — **godseffiana** (green edged with white) and **musaica** (red, orange and copper).

leaves reddish when young

leaf 3 in. long

CLEYERA JAPONICA TRICOLOR

An unusual shrub which grows about 2 ft tall — you will certainly not find it at your local garden centre. Sometimes sold as **Eurya japonica** it is easy to grow and its glossy variegated leaves are attractive.

Cleyera japonica variegata

● PEPEROMIAS

Bushy species

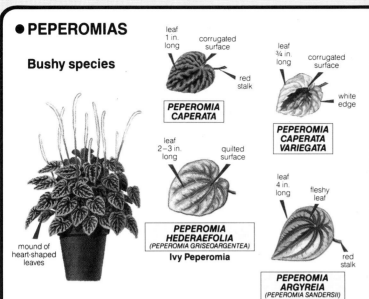

mound of
heart-shaped
leaves

leaf
1 in.
long

corrugated
surface

red
stalk

**PEPEROMIA
CAPERATA**

leaf
¾ in.
long

corrugated
surface

white
edge

**PEPEROMIA
CAPERATA
VARIEGATA**

leaf
2–3 in.
long

quilted
surface

**PEPEROMIA
HEDERAEFOLIA**
(PEPEROMIA GRISEOARGENTEA)
Ivy Peperomia

leaf
4 in.
long

fleshy
leaf

red
stalk

**PEPEROMIA
ARGYREIA**
(PEPEROMIA SANDERSII)
Watermelon Peperomia

Peperomia caperata variegata

Peperomias are widely used in dish gardens, bottle gardens and situations where space is limited. They are slow growing, compact and many produce curious 'rat-tail' flower-heads. The bushy Peperomias grow about 4–6 in. high, and the familiar small-leaved species is **P. caperata**. Dwarf varieties such as **Little Fantasy** and the white-edged **variegata** are available. There are several out-of-the-ordinary small-leaved bushes — **P. orba Astrid** bears pale green, spoon-shaped leaves and **P. fraseri** stands out from other Peperomias by producing round and sweetly-scented flower-heads. The large-leaved bushes are more popular — you will have no trouble in finding the metallic-leaved **P. hederaefolia**, but the striped-leaved **P. argyreia** is harder to find in the shops than in the books.

The upright Peperomias have more distinct stems which grow vertically for part or all of the plant's life. Unfortunately there is much confusion over naming — the textbooks and the plant labels rarely agree! The small fleshy-leaved variety blotched with yellow is **P. glabella variegata** — much more popular is the large-leaved **P. magnoliaefolia**. The other fleshy-leaved varieties on upright stems are all types of the Baby Rubber Plant — **P. obtusifolia** has all-green leaves, **P. Green Gold** has yellow-blotched leaves and **P. clusiifolia** has all-green leaves edged with purple. **P. verticillata** is unmistakable (1 ft stems with whorls of leaves) and so is **P. pereskiaefolia** — look for the zig-zagged stems.

Peperomia argyreia

Upright species

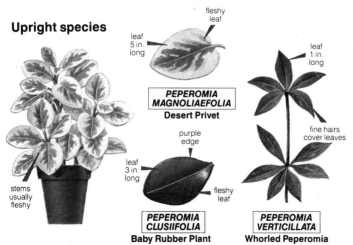

stems
usually
fleshy

fleshy
leaf

leaf
5 in.
long

**PEPEROMIA
MAGNOLIAEFOLIA**
Desert Privet

purple
edge

leaf
3 in.
long

fleshy
leaf

**PEPEROMIA
CLUSIIFOLIA**
Baby Rubber Plant

leaf
1 in.
long

fine hairs
cover leaves

**PEPEROMIA
VERTICILLATA**
Whorled Peperomia

Peperomia magnoliaefolia

Bushy Plants

Hypoestes sanguinolenta Splash

leaf
2 in.
long

pink
spots

HYPOESTES SANGUINOLENTA

Freckle Face
(Polka Dot Plant)

The downy leaves of **Hypoestes sanguinolenta (H. phyllostachya)** are covered with pale pink spots — they are at their showiest in the variety **Splash**. Pinch out tips to maintain bushiness. Flowers are insignificant.

leaf
3 in.
long

wine
red
leaves

IRESINE HERBSTII

Bloodleaf
(Beefsteak Plant)

The Iresines are widely grown in the U.S. but not in Britain. Bloodleaf grows about 2 ft high, its red stems bearing notched leaves. **I. herbstii aureo-reticulata** (Chicken Gizzard) is more colourful — red stems, green leaves and yellow veins.

Iresine herbstii aureoreticulata

Aucuba japonica variegata

leaf
5 in.
long

serrated
leaves

AUCUBA JAPONICA VARIEGATA

Spotted Laurel

A. japonica is an outdoor shrub which will grow to about 3 ft indoors. The leathery leaves are glossy and only the variegated types are used. **Variegata** is the most popular — **goldiana** (almost all-yellow) is the most colourful.

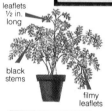

leaflets
½ in.
long

leaf
5 in.
long

black
stems

filmy
leaflets

ADIANTUM RADDIANUM
(ADIANTUM CUNEATUM)

Maidenhair Fern

The Maidenhair Ferns are easy to recognise — look for the triangular leaflets and wiry stems. Several species are grown, such as **A. capillus-veneris** and the larger **A. tenerum**. The favourite one is **A. raddianum fragrans**.

Adiantum capillus-veneris

Pseuderanthemum kewense

glossy
variegated
leaves

leaf
5 in.
long

PSEUDERANTHEMUM KEWENSE
(ERANTHEMUM ATROPURPUREUM)

A colourful but straggly shrub which can grow 3 ft high. The leaves are marked with purple, and varieties such as **tricolor** and **variegatum** are splashed with white, cream and pink. Mature plants bear red-spotted white flowers in spring.

leaf
4 in.
long

leathery
leaves

GEOGENANTHUS UNDATUS

Seersucker Plant

A compact plant, rarely exceeding 10 in. The oval fleshy leaves bear prominent silvery stripes and the surface is puckered — hence the common name. Mauve flowers may appear in summer, but Geogenanthus is grown for its foliage.

Geogenanthus undatus

● COLEUS

stems square in cross section

saw-edged leaves

COLEUS BLUMEI
Flame Nettle

COLEUS BLUMEI SCARLET RAINBOW

COLEUS BLUMEI KLONDYKE

COLEUS BLUMEI CANDIDUM

COLEUS BLUMEI FIREBIRD

COLEUS BLUMEI VOLCANO

Coleus Salmon Lace

Coleus plants have two outstanding features — they are colourful and they are cheap. The usual plan is to buy (or raise) young plants in spring and keep them until winter arrives. The standard height is 1–2 ft, but dwarf varieties such as **Sabre** are available. New plants are raised from seed or cuttings and there is a bewildering choice of **Coleus blumei** hybrids. Most (but not all) have nettle-like leaves — there are also ruffled ones (e.g **The Chief**), frilly ones (e.g **Firebird**) and wavy-edged ones (e.g **Butterfly**). There is no basic colour — almost every conceivable mixture can be found. There are some attractive single-coloured varieties, such as **Golden Bedder** (yellow) and **Volcano** (deep red), but the usual choice is for a multicoloured Coleus. Take care — a rainbow of foliage colour may look attractive in an outdoor bed but can look garish indoors. Remove the stem tips occasionally.

Coleus Sabre Mixed

Dracaena godseffiana Florida Beauty

glossy leaves

leaf 3 in. long

wiry stems

DRACAENA GODSEFFIANA
Gold Dust Dracaena

Dracaena godseffiana is quite different from the palm-like Dracaenas (pages 33–34) which are so popular. It is a much-branched shrub with laurel-like leaves. The foliage is spotted with cream — the amount depends on the variety. The leaves of **Florida Beauty** are more cream than green.

leaf 2 in. long

leathery leaves

EUONYMUS JAPONICA MEDIOPICTUS

Euonymus is a garden shrub which can be grown indoors — E. japonica is the species used. There are several varieties which grow about 4 ft high, differing in the distribution of green and yellow (or white) on the leaves. Grow the dwarf **E. japonica microphyllus** where space is limited.

Euonymus japonica microphyllus albus

Trees

Foliage Trees are an extremely important group of house plants, providing spectacular specimens for large displays and the basic centrepiece in more modest displays. All Trees have the same basic form — a single stem which may be branched or unbranched above the lower trunk and which bears non-succulent foliage with relatively small leaf bases. The dividing line between Trees and Bushy Plants is not quite as clear-cut as this textbook definition — some Trees, such as Coffea, may produce several main stems with age, whereas one or two Bushy Plants (e.g Alocasia) may occasionally have only a single stem.

Flowering and Fruiting Trees are described in other chapters, and not all Foliage Trees are listed in this section — some have distinctive leaf forms and are therefore to be found on earlier pages. Examples are Araucaria (page 28), Dizygotheca (page 11), Grevillea (page 28), Heptapleurum (page 11) and Schefflera (page 11).

● CODIAEUMS

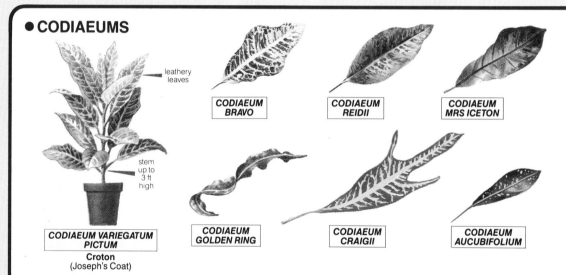

leathery leaves

CODIAEUM BRAVO

CODIAEUM REIDII

CODIAEUM MRS ICETON

stem up to 3 ft high

CODIAEUM VARIEGATUM PICTUM
Croton
(Joseph's Coat)

CODIAEUM GOLDEN RING

CODIAEUM CRAIGII

CODIAEUM AUCUBIFOLIUM

Codiaeum Norma

The Crotons are bought for their colourful foliage — brilliant reds, yellows and greens in various shapes. The basic variety is **C. variegatum pictum**, and over the years hundreds of different named types have appeared. Most have laurel-like foliage, but there are also forked leaves, long ribbons, lobed leaves, twisted and curled types. Identification is not easy — the colour often changes with age, a pink or red hue taking over from the yellows and greens. Examples of well-known varieties include **Appleleaf** and **Vulcan** (yellow with red edges and green veins), **Norma** (green with red veins and splashes of yellow), **aucubifolium** (green with yellow spots), **Bravo** (green splashed with yellow and red). **Reidii** is popular — so are the lobed varieties such as **craigii** and **holuffiana**. There are many, many others, such as **Mrs Iceton, Excellent, Gold Finger, Gold Sun** and **Julietta**.

Codiaeum Gold Finger

● FICUS

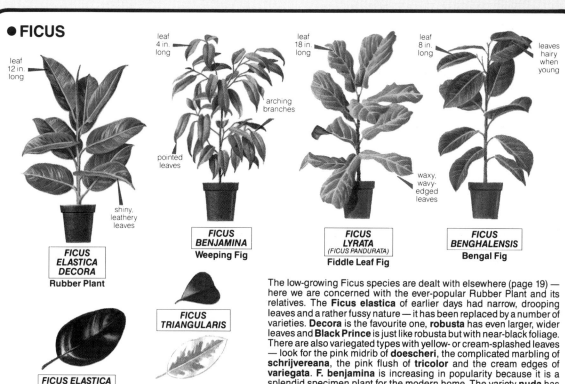

leaf 12 in. long

shiny, leathery leaves

FICUS ELASTICA DECORA
Rubber Plant

leaf 4 in. long

arching branches

pointed leaves

FICUS BENJAMINA
Weeping Fig

leaf 18 in. long

waxy, wavy-edged leaves

FICUS LYRATA
(FICUS PANDURATA)
Fiddle Leaf Fig

leaf 8 in. long

leaves hairy when young

FICUS BENGHALENSIS
Bengal Fig

FICUS ELASTICA BLACK PRINCE

FICUS TRIANGULARIS

FICUS RUBIGINOSA VARIEGATA
Rusty Fig

FICUS ELASTICA TRICOLOR

FICUS RELIGIOSA
Bo Tree

The low-growing Ficus species are dealt with elsewhere (page 19) — here we are concerned with the ever-popular Rubber Plant and its relatives. The **Ficus elastica** of earlier days had narrow, drooping leaves and a rather fussy nature — it has been replaced by a number of varieties. **Decora** is the favourite one, **robusta** has even larger, wider leaves and **Black Prince** is just like robusta but with near-black foliage. There are also variegated types with yellow- or cream-splashed leaves — look for the pink midrib of **doescheri**, the complicated marbling of **schrijvereana**, the pink flush of **tricolor** and the cream edges of **variegata**. F. benjamina is increasing in popularity because it is a splendid specimen plant for the modern home. The variety **nuda** has narrow leaves — other varieties include **Hawaii**, **Starlight** and **Gold Princess**. F. benjamina is a weeping tree growing about 6 ft high — **F. rubiginosa (F. australis)** is a low-spreading tree with 4 in. long leaves. Its common name (Rusty Fig) is derived from the brown colouration of the underside of the leaves. Other species with 3-4 in. leaves include **F. triangularis** (triangular), **F. retusa** (oval) and **F. religiosa** (heart-shaped with a tail-like tip). Even smaller is the foliage of the shrub-like **F. buxifolia** — the brown stems bear 1 in. triangular leaves. But the spectacular species are the large-leaved ones — **F. benghalensis** (the Banyan Tree of India) bears leaves of the standard Rubber Plant type but which are hairy when young. The largest-leaved popular Ficus is **F. lyrata** — violin-like foliage in both shape and size.

Ficus elastica robusta

Ficus benjamina variegata

Ficus elastica schrijvereana

●OTHER TREES

leaflet 3 in. across

leathery leaves

POLYSCIAS BALFOURIANA
Dinner Plate Aralia

leaf 8 in. long

feathery leaves

POLYSCIAS FRUTICOSA
Ming Aralia

leaf 3 in. long

strap-like leaves

PODOCARPUS MACROPHYLLUS
Buddhist Pine

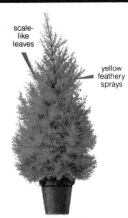

scale-like leaves

yellow feathery sprays

CUPRESSUS MACROCARPA GOLDCREST

leaf 6 in. long

wavy-edged leaves

COFFEA ARABICA
Coffee Tree

Polyscias is a much-branched tree bearing twisted stems and decorative foliage. The most popular one is **P. balfouriana** with dark green, rounded leaflets which are speckled with grey or pale green. The variety **pennockii** is yellow-veined — **marginata** has white-bordered foliage. **P. fruticosa** is quite different — the leaves are much longer and are divided into many irregular and saw-edged leaflets.

Polyscias guilfoylei is sometimes called Wild Coffee — the true Coffee Tree (**Coffea arabica**) can be grown indoors, reaching about 4 ft high and under good conditions producing white fragrant flowers and red fruit. If you want flowers and fruit rather than a large tree, choose the variety **nana**. Coffee is more familiar in the kitchen than growing in the living room — so is Avocado, but **Persea americana** can be grown quite easily from a stone to produce a small tree with attractive, pale green foliage.

Podocarpus is an Oriental conifer — the species **P. macrophyllus** is grown for its strap-like, glossy leaves. Few conifers of the traditional type are grown indoors — look for the upright **Cupressus macrocarpa Goldcrest** or the weeping **C. cashmeriana**.

Stereospermum chelonoides (listed as **Radermachera**) has recently appeared in the shops. Interesting, but relatively untried.

leaf 4 in. long

leathery leaves

PERSEA AMERICANA
Avocado Tree

Coffea arabica

Stereospermum chelonoides

Cupressus cashmeriana

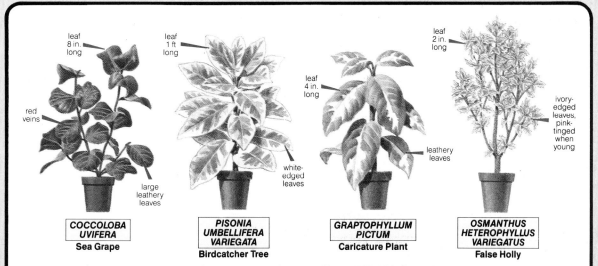

COCCOLOBA UVIFERA
Sea Grape

leaf 8 in. long

red veins

large leathery leaves

PISONIA UMBELLIFERA VARIEGATA
Birdcatcher Tree

leaf 1 ft long

white-edged leaves

GRAPTOPHYLLUM PICTUM
Caricature Plant

leaf 4 in. long

leathery leaves

OSMANTHUS HETEROPHYLLUS VARIEGATUS
False Holly

leaf 2 in. long

ivory-edged leaves, pink-tinged when young

leaf 3 in long

aromatic leaves

LAURUS NOBILIS
Bay Tree

If at first glance you can't tell a Pisonia leaf from a variegated Rubber Plant one, never mind — neither can the experts. The growth habit, however, is rather different. The stems readily branch and the leaves bear a sticky resin — hence the common name. Another unusual plant is **Graptophyllum pictum** — at the centre of each oval leaf is an irregularly-shaped white blotch. Occasionally (and fancifully) this blotch looks like a human face, so both this plant and the previous one derive their names from a feature of the foliage.

Osmanthus heterophyllus variegatus looks like Variegated Holly but it is a much better choice for growing indoors. The prickly leaves are edged with creamy-white and are tinged with pink when young — the tree will grow about 3 ft tall. Bay Trees reach about the same height when grown in a sunny spot indoors — these decorative plants are a common sight outdoors but are rarely listed as house plants.

Coccoloba uvifera is commonly grown in semi-tropical regions but is not often seen indoors. A good choice for the lover of rarities — stiff, olive green leaves with prominent veins. You will have no trouble in finding a Eucalyptus, cultivated for its grey-green or grey-blue foliage. **E. globulus** soon grows too tall — a better choice is **E. gunnii** or **E. citriodora**.

leaf 2 in. long

aromatic leaves

EUCALYPTUS GLOBULUS
Blue Gum

Laurus nobilis

Osmanthus heterophyllus variegatus

Eucalyptus gunnii

CHAPTER 3
SPINY-STEMMED HOUSE PLANTS

Nearly all the Spiny-stemmed Plants are cacti. This large and extremely popular group has evolved from primitive types which looked more like roses than the familiar globes and columns which we know today. One of these ancestral cacti still exists and is grown as a house plant — see Pereskia on page 68.

A few plants with stems which are distinctly spined but are not cacti are included here — there are several Euphorbias and the much rarer Pachypodium. In addition there are several plants which bear occasional spines or thorns on their stems. Examples include Citrus, Fortunella and Rosa, and they are described elsewhere in this book.

● NON-CACTI

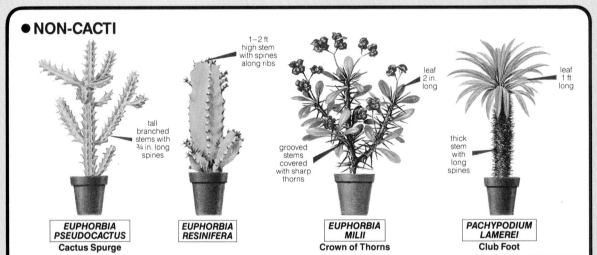

1–2 ft high stem with spines along ribs

leaf 2 in. long

leaf 1 ft long

tall branched stems with ¾ in. long spines

grooved stems covered with sharp thorns

thick stem with long spines

EUPHORBIA PSEUDOCACTUS	EUPHORBIA RESINIFERA	EUPHORBIA MILII	PACHYPODIUM LAMEREI
Cactus Spurge		Crown of Thorns	Club Foot

Euphorbia grandicornis

There are several Euphorbia species which are indistinguishable from cacti — only the milky sap within reveals their non-cactus nature. Examples of these Euphorbias are **E. pseudocactus** (ridged candelabra-like stems 5 ft high when mature), **E. grandicornis** (rather similar but with twisted and gnarled stems), **E. resinifera** (fat stems with 4 shallow ribs) and **E. horrida** (columnar stems with deep ribs and fierce spines). The Crown of Thorns (**E. milii**) is much more popular than the cactus-like Euphorbias — its 3 ft stems bear tiny flowers surrounded by showy red bracts from early spring until midsummer. Several varieties are available — red is the usual flower-head colour but both salmon and yellow types are available.

Pachypodium lamerei is a rarity from Madagascar. Although you may never see one, its tall cactus-like stem does show that not all the false cacti are Euphorbias.

Euphorbia milii

● CACTI

slender green stems and brown spines. Pink tubular flowers

globular white-flaked stem with prominent ribs and curved spines

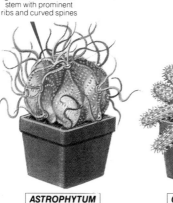

finger-like stems and white spines

grey-green columnar stem covered with long silvery hairs

APOROCACTUS FLAGELLIFORMIS
Rat's Tail Cactus

ASTROPHYTUM CAPRICORNE
Goat's Horn Cactus

CHAMAECEREUS SILVESTRII
Peanut Cactus

CEPHALOCEREUS SENILIS
Old Man Cactus

columnar stem with prominent ribs and brown spines

distorted branched stems with irregular ribs

Aporocactus flagelliformis is a popular and easy cactus — the ½ in. wide stems grow several inches each year and the 3 in. long flowers appear in spring. Good for hanging baskets, but remember that the ⅛ in. spines are sharp. **A. mallisonii** (**Heliaporus smithii**) is similar but the stems are thicker, the spines longer and the flowers larger.

Astrophytum begins life as a ribbed ball but becomes cylindrical with age. Yellow daisy-like flowers are produced in summer on mature plants, which grow 6–12 in. tall depending on the species. **Astrophytum capricorne** has curved spines, **A. ornatum** (Star Cactus) bears long straight spines and **A. myriostigma** (Bishop's Cap) has no spines at all.

Chamaecereus silvestrii is an old favourite — it spreads rapidly, the 3 in. long stems readily producing red flowers in early summer. If you think that cacti never bloom, grow this one.

On the other hand **Cephalocereus senilis** will never flower indoors. It is grown for its columnar stem which reaches about 1 ft and is completely covered by 5 in. long hairs.

Cereus peruvianus is the pride of many a collection — the stem reaching 2–3 ft in time and bearing 6 in. long flowers in summer. **C. jamacaru** is quite similar, but the spines are yellow and the white, night-opening flowers are even longer. **C. peruvianus monstrosus** is a slow-growing grotesque mutant.

CEREUS PERUVIANUS
Column Cactus

CEREUS PERUVIANUS MONSTROSUS
Rock Cactus

Aporocactus flagelliformis

Cereus jamacaru

Astrophytum ornatum

● CACTI continued

globular, wavy-ribbed stem and long spines

ECHINOFOSSULOCACTUS ZACATECASENSIS
Brain Cactus

globular ribbed stem and sharp yellow spines

ECHINOCACTUS GRUSONII
Barrel Cactus

small, globular dark green stem and small spines

ECHINOCEREUS KNIPPELIANUS

columnar stem with numerous ribs and small comb-like spines

ECHINOCEREUS PECTINATUS
Hedgehog Cactus

The convoluted ribs of Echinofossulocactus are almost as complex as its name — fortunately the ball-like Brain Cactus is usually sold as Stenocactus. There are several species — **E. multicostatus**, **E. hastatus**, **E. zacatecasensis** etc, and the usual form is a 6 in. globe with 1 in. spines.

Echinocactus is a slow-growing ball — it will take 10 years or more to reach a diameter of 9 in. **E. grusonii** is the common one — there is a golden crown of woolly hairs at the top and prominent spines along the ribs. It will not flower indoors — for deep pink flowers grow **E. horizonthalonius**.

There are many species of Echinocereus and some confusion over their names. The column-like one covered with spines is either **E. pectinatus** or the very similar **E. rigidissimus**. Height is about 10 in. and the pink flowers are scented. The much smaller **E. knippelianus** is more ball-like and less spiny. **E. salm-dyckianus** produces bright orange flowers.

The Cleistocacti are slow-growing, tall and densely covered with spines. Flowering does not begin until the plants are many years old, and the tubular flowers only partly open. **C. straussii** is the favourite species, reaching 4 ft or more after several decades. The wool and spines are white, giving the plant a silvery appearance.

Espostoa, like Cephalocereus, is a densely hairy species — the main difference is the presence of sharp spines on Espostoa. **E. lanata** is the only one you are likely to find — a 1–2 ft column which does not bloom indoors. **E. melanostele** is white at first, but later the hairs turn black.

slender many-ribbed columnar stem covered with fine white bristles

CLEISTOCACTUS STRAUSSII
Silver Torch Cactus

columnar stem covered with silky white hairs

ESPOSTOA LANATA
Snowball Cactus

Echinocactus horizonthalonius

Echinocereus salm-dyckianus

Espostoa melanostele

globular or short columnar stem and short spines

ECHINOPSIS EYRIESII
Sea Urchin Cactus

globular or columnar stem and long spines

ECHINOPSIS RHODOTRICHA
Sea Urchin Cactus

grey-green globular stem with prominent ribs and large red hooked spines

FEROCACTUS LATISPINUS
Fish Hook Cactus

brightly-coloured stem grafted on to another cactus stock

GYMNOCALYCIUM MIHANOVICHII FRIEDRICHII
Hibotan Cactus

columnar stem and dense cover of yellow spines

HAAGEOCEREUS CHOSICENSIS

globular or short columnar stem. Flowers followed by red fruits

HAMATOCACTUS SETISPINUS
Strawberry Cactus

There is nothing special about the ball-like or oval stems of Echinopsis — the notable feature is the outstanding floral display which appears each summer. **E. eyriesii** is the popular one, bearing ¼ in. brown spines on prominent ribs — the 6 in. long flowers are scented. The large Sea Urchin Cactus is **E. rhodotricha** which bears 1 in. spines and scentless flowers.

Ferocactus is a fearsome plant — barrel-shaped and armed with stout spines. The red bristles of **F. latispinus** are hooked -- hence the common name. This cactus rarely blooms indoors — for orange flowers in summer grow **F. acanthodes**.

Gymnocalycium is the Chin Cactus, and most species and varieties are rather ordinary. The small globular bodies are green, ribbed and spined, but there is one group which are entirely red or yellow. These strains of **G. mihanovichii friedrichii** are the Hibotan or Red Cap Cacti — their brightly-coloured stems lack chlorophyll and so are grafted on to a green cactus.

Most of the cacti in this chapter are reasonably common, but Haageocereus appears in few shops and even fewer textbooks. The basic species is **H. chosicensis** — a broadly columnar cactus with the green surface hidden by bristle-like spines.

Hamatocactus setispinus is a close relative of Ferocactus — there are prominent ribs and large hooked spines. The ribs, however, are curved and notched, and the yellow blooms are readily produced each summer.

Echinopsis rhodotricha

Ferocactus acanthodes

Gymnocalycium mihanovichii friedrichii

● CACTI continued

globular stem
with many ribs
and pale
brown spines

| **LOBIVIA AUREA** |
| Golden Lily Cactus |

columnar
stem with
many ribs
and yellow
spreading
spines

| **LOBIVIA FAMATIMENSIS** |
| Sunset Cactus |

globular stem
with hooked
spines and dense
white hairs

| **MAMMILLARIA BOCASANA** |
| Powder Puff Cactus |

short columnar
stem with
prominent
tubercles
and hooked
spines

| **MAMMILLARIA WILDII** |

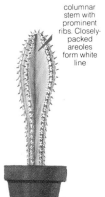

columnar
stem with
prominent
ribs. Closely-
packed
areoles
form white
line

| **LEMAIREOCEREUS MARGINATUS** |
| Organ Pipe Cactus |

Lobivia is a good cactus for the beginner — it remains compact (3–6 in. high) and readily produces red or yellow blooms. Several species are available — the oval **L. famatimensis** is covered with flat yellow bristles and bears large golden flowers. Both **L. aurea** and **L. hertrichiana** are ball-shaped with prominent ribs and the summer blooms measure several inches in diameter.

Any large collection of cacti will contain several Mammillaria species and varieties. Their popularity is based on the compact growth habit and their free-flowering nature even when quite young — many bear attractive fruits once the small flowers have faded. One of the recognition features is the presence of tubercles in place of ribs, each tubercle bearing spines at the apex. The favourite species is **M. bocasana** — a cluster-forming silvery plant which bears a ring of small white blooms around the stem in spring. The oval-shaped **M. wildii** is quite similar — **M. rhodantha** and **M. hahniana** bear pink flowers.

In contrast to Lobivia and Mammillaria, Lemaireocereus is not easy to grow and often succumbs to disease. It is one of the much-branched cacti seen in Western films, growing 20 ft or more, but in the home **L. marginatus** is usually a single column with dense white wool along the ribs to tell you that it is not a Cereus (page 63). **Myrtillocactus geometrizans** is an unusual type, with stems which branch and turn blue with age. **Heliocereus speciosus** (Sun Cactus) is another odd one — its green stems branch at the base and trail downwards. Bright red flowers appear in early summer.

branched
columnar
stem with
prominent
ribs and
long spines

| **MYRTILLOCACTUS GEOMETRIZANS** |
| Blue Myrtle Cactus |

Lobivia hertrichiana

Mammillaria hahniana

Heliocereus speciosus

oval pads with long yellow spines

OPUNTIA BERGERIANA

oval pads with tufts of golden bristles

OPUNTIA MICRODASYS
Bunny Ears

globular stem with yellow bristly spines

PARODIA CHRYSACANTHION

globular stem with red hooked spines

PARODIA SANGUINIFLORA
Tom Thumb Cactus

columnar stem with yellow spines. Flat top slopes towards sun

NOTOCACTUS LENINGHAUSII
Golden Ball Cactus

Opuntias come in all sizes, ranging from prostrate plants no taller than a mouse to towering trees as high as an elephant. The most popular ones bear flattened pads and are the Prickly Pears of tropical regions, although they rarely fruit indoors. The favourite Opuntia is **O. microdasys** which grows about 1 ft tall and bears groups of tiny hooked barbs known as glochids. In the variety **albinospina** they are white — in **O. rufida** (Red Bunny Ears) they are brown. Many different Opuntias are available as house plants — grow the long-spined **O. bergeriana** if you want flowers, **O. brasiliensis** if you want a tall, tree-like plant or choose **O. cylindrica** if you want a column-like Opuntia which your friends won't be able to recognise.

Like Mammillarias, the Parodias are small, ball-like cacti which are tubercled rather than ribbed and which bear flowers from an early age. Unlike Mammillarias, they are usually solitary plants which do not readily form a large number of offsets at the base. The red-flowering one is **P. sanguiniflora** — the yellow-flowering types are **P. aureispina** (Golden Tom Thumb Cactus) which bears hooked spines and **P. chrysacanthion** which has bristle-like spines.

Notocactus has the common name Ball Cactus because the globular shape is not lost, although some species change to an oval form with age. **N. ottonis** is a typical Notocactus — spherical, fiercely spined and bearing 3 in. wide yellow flowers on plants which are only a few years old. **N. apricus** is another yellow-flowering ball-like type, but **N. leninghausii** is grown for its columnar stem rather than its blooms.

globular stem with spreading red spines

NOTOCACTUS OTTONIS
Ball Cactus

Opuntia rufida

Parodia aureispina

Notocactus leninghausii

● CACTI continued

columnar stem with yellow spines and long white hairs

OREOCEREUS CELSIANUS
Old Man of the Andes

globular stems and short white spines

REBUTIA MINISCULA
Mexican Sunball

finger-like stems and tiny spines

REBUTIA PYGMAEA

columnar stem with large areoles and long yellow spines

TRICHOCEREUS CANDICANS
Torch Cactus

semi-evergreen shrub with spiny stems and green leaves

PERESKIA ACULEATA
Rose Cactus

semi-evergreen shrub with spiny stems and leaves red on underside

PERESKIA GODSEFFIANA
Rose Cactus

Oreocereus celsianus is an oval cactus bearing white hairs and a woolly top — the common name of this plant from the S. American mountains seems quite appropriate. With age the yellow spines turn red, branches arise from the base and red flowers appear. **O. trollii** is a less common species which is smaller and bears fewer ribs.

Rebutia is a popular cactus because it is small and starts to flower while still quite young. It is similar to Mammillaria in many ways — the globular stems are covered with tubercles rather than ribs and offsets are readily produced at the base. The bright funnel-shaped flowers, however, are borne close to the base rather than as a ring around the top as occurs with so many Mammillarias. **R. miniscula** is the favourite one — 2 in. balls bearing orange or pink flowers in early summer. The variety **grandiflora** bears large red blooms — **violaciflora** produces mauve ones. The baby is **R. pygmaea** (less than 1 in. high) and the giants are **R. kupperiana** and **R. senilis** (3–4 in. high).

Trichocereus is the Torch Cactus, grown for its columnar stems and huge white flowers which are borne on mature plants. **T. candicans** branches freely and grows about 3 ft tall — the more popular **T. spachianus** forms an impressive bristly column reaching 5 ft or more.

The odd man out — Pereskia bears thin spiny stems and true leaves. The flowers look like wild roses — hence the common name. **P. aculeata** is the common one, growing to 6 ft — the golden-leaved **P. godseffiana** is attractive but hard to find.

Oreocereus celsianus

Rebutia senilis

Pereskia aculeata

CHAPTER 4
FRUITING HOUSE PLANTS

Some textbooks paint far too rosy a picture of the living room as a growing area for fresh fruit for the table. Sweet oranges, luscious limes, pomegranates, lemons, pineapples, bananas ... all are considered possible in the well-lit room.

In reality you require skill, time, plenty of space and a greenhouse or conservatory to succeed with tropical fruits for culinary use. In the average room pineapples rarely ripen, oranges remain small and bitter, pomegranates fall off the plant shortly after they have formed and juicy bananas remain just a dream. This is not a book on indoor vegetable growing, but there are several vegetable fruits which can be grown on the large windowsill and they are described on these first two pages. Very welcome — but rather less exotic than the tropical fruits promised in some catalogues.

The more popular fruiting plants are grown for the decorative nature of their fruits, and the most popular ones are illustrated and described on pages 71–73. A few fruiting plants are described elsewhere in this book — examples are Coffea arabica (page 60) and Hamatocactus setispinus (page 65).

● FRUIT FOR KITCHEN USE

Tomato Minibel

Cucumber Fembaby

Aubergine Long Purple

Once the idea of growing the Tomato (**Lycopersicon esculentum**) as a house plant was unthinkable, but the introduction of bushy dwarfs such as **Florida Petit, Minibel** and **Tiny Tim** now make it possible. Follow the standard rules — water daily when necessary, feed regularly, stake if required and tap the stems to aid pollination. Clusters of cherry-sized delicious fruit will be your reward.

Cucumber (**Cucumis sativus**) sounds even less like a house plant, but the F_1 hybrid **Fembaby** has brought this greenhouse crop into the home. The plants grow no more than 3 ft high and are easily trained. The yellow flowers are all-female and each one should produce a cucumber. Stand the pot on a windowsill in a saucer and keep topped up with water. Mist leaves daily.

The Aubergine (**Solanum melongena ovigerum**) makes an excellent windowsill plant, growing about 1 ft high. Pinch out the tips if the stems exceed this height — stake as necessary and mist the leaves regularly. Grow **Easter Egg** for white fruits, **Long Purple** for the standard Eggplant of the supermarket or **Black Enorma** (1 lb. or more) to impress the neighbours.

● FRUIT FOR KITCHEN USE continued

Peanut

Strawberry

Sweet Pepper

The Peanut or Groundnut (**Arachis hypogaea**) is an annual grown by planting unshelled and unroasted peanuts. The result is a rather plain 1 ft high plant with oval leaflets and short-lived yellow flowers borne just above soil level. Nothing special — but after the flowers have faded there is the extraordinary growth habit of stalks which curve downwards and drive the developing fruits into the compost. Warm conditions are essential.

You can grow ordinary strawberries in tubs or clay strawberry pots indoors, but it is usually better to choose the more compact Alpine Strawberry (**Fragaria vesca sempervirens**). It is easily raised from seed and the small plant (there are no runners) will produce its first fruits about 4 or 5 months after germination. Choose **Alexandria** for the largest berries.

The varieties of **Capsicum annuum** grown indoors are nearly always the small-fruited Christmas Pepper (page 73) used to brighten up the winter windowsill. But there are also the large-fruited Sweet Peppers, which are picked at the green or red stage for cooking. You will need a large well-lit area — they grow 2–3 ft high. Insects love them, which can make them a poor indoor plant. Suitable varieties include **Canape** and **Gypsy**.

Mushroom

Okra

Kumquat

The Mushroom (**Psalliota campestris**) may seem a strange choice for a book on indoor plants, but it is a fruit-bearing plant which is easily grown in an ordinary room and so earns its place here. Buy a Mushroom Tub — they are readily available and everything will have been done for you. No special care is needed — the upper surface or casing is kept moist and the first buttons will appear in 4–6 weeks.

Okra (**Hibiscus esculentus**) has begun to appear in the supermarkets — 4 in. long pods used in soups, stews and curries. Seeds are now sold by large nurseries and it is generally grown in the greenhouse. Although you won't find it in the house plant books you can grow it in a sunny spot indoors. You will need space — the plants grow about 3ft high, but there are no pests to worry about and the pretty yellow flowers and erect pods provide a conversation piece.

The Kumquat is the one member of the Citrus family which can be relied upon to bear edible fruit under well-lit but ordinary room conditions. **Fortunella margarita** (Nagami Kumquat) bears oval orange fruit which are about 1½ in. long and are eaten whole. The glossy leaves are about 4 in. long — the spring and summer sweetly-scented white flowers are followed by the fruit in autumn.

● FRUIT FOR DECORATION

Aechmea fulgens discolor

purple flowers; red berries

underside purple

AECHMEA FULGENS DISCOLOR
Coral Berry

Aechmeas are generally grown for their leaves (page 37) or flowers (page 101) — **Aechmea fulgens discolor** is grown mainly for its display of berries which remain on the plant for several months.

fruit aromatic but not usually edible

leaves stiff and spiny

stalk 2–3 ft high

ANANAS COMOSUS VARIEGATUS
Ivory Pineapple

The Common Pineapple (**Ananas comosus**) and its yellow-striped form **variegatus** will produce pink flowers on mature plants. These are followed by small pink fruits if the plants have been kept under warm and humid conditions.

Ananas comosus variegatus

creamy flowers followed by round white fruits

pale green stems

RHIPSALIS CASSUTHA
Mistletoe Cactus

In its natural habitat **Rhipsalis cassutha** hangs from trees — indoors its long, branching stems trail over the rim of the pot. Small flowers are produced in summer and the fruits which appear later have a mistletoe-like appearance.

Rhipsalis burchellii

small olive-like berries

leathery, dark green leaves

FICUS DIVERSIFOLIA
Mistletoe Fig

Ficus diversifolia (**F. deltoidea**) is a slow-growing bush, eventually reaching a height of about 3 ft. The leaves bear small brown spots and the pea-sized fruits appear all year round — quite attractive but inedible.

Ficus diversifolia

Ardisia crenata

stem 3 ft high

fragrant flowers followed by red berries

ARDISIA CRENATA
Coral Berry

A handsome tree, sometimes labelled as **Ardisia crispa**. The 6 in. long leaves are oval and leathery, and the white or pale pink flowers are followed by clusters of berries which remain on the plant for months.

creeping stems with tiny leaves. Glassy orange berries cover surface in autumn

NERTERA DEPRESSA
Bead Plant

The mat of creeping stems and ¼ in. leaves might be mistaken for Helxine (see page 19) at first glance, but once the tiny greenish flowers have faded in summer the dense cover of pea-sized berries makes this plant immediately recognisable.

Nertera depressa

● FRUIT FOR DECORATION continued

leaf 2 in. long with wavy edges

star-shaped flowers followed by roundish-oval berries

downy stems

SOLANUM CAPSICASTRUM
Winter Cherry

Solanum pseudocapsicum

The Winter Cherry (**Solanum capsicastrum**) is sold in vast quantities every Christmas from supermarkets, garden centres and market stalls. The dark green leaves are narrowly oval and the white flowers form berries which are about ½ in. in diameter when mature. The plants are usually bought when the fruits have changed from green to orange-red and these will remain on the plants for months if kept in a cool place. There are several varieties, such as **Cherry Ripe** (bright red berries) and **variegatum** (cream-splashed leaves). The Jerusalem Cherry (**S. pseudocapsicum**) is also popular, especially in the U.S., and is quite similar. If you look closely, however, you will see that the stems are smooth. Also the berries are larger, the leaves shorter and the colours generally brighter. The species is quite tall (1½–2½ ft) but 1 ft dwarf varieties (**nanum**, **Tom Thumb**, etc) are the favourite types.

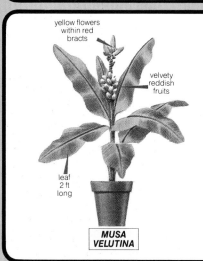

yellow flowers within red bracts

velvety reddish fruits

leaf 2 ft long

MUSA VELUTINA

Musa coccinea

A banana plant provides a tropical look to any conservatory, but the Common Banana (**Musa paradisiaca**) and many other species and varieties are far too large to grow. Perhaps the best one for growing in a large tub is **M. acuminata cavendishii** — the Canary Island or Dwarf Banana. It grows about 6 ft high and its tubular flowers are followed by typical bananas . . . if you have been able to provide the light, warmth and high humidity required. Bananas are best regarded as decorative rather than productive plants indoors. **M. velutina** grows about 4 ft high — the yellow flowers are followed by attractive but inedible fruit. Even smaller is **M. coccinea**, the Flowering Banana. The plant grows 3 ft high and the ornamental bananas are only 2 in. long.

leathery leaf 3 in. long

white fragrant flowers followed by small fruit — flowers and fruit appear all year round

CITRUS MITIS
Calamondin Orange

Citrus limon

You can raise plants by sowing orange, lemon or lime pips but they cannot be expected to flower and fruit. The trouble is that most types of Citrus will not fruit until they are too large for an ordinary room. There are a few dwarfs which can be relied upon to form oranges or lemons indoors, but you will have to provide good conditions and even then you cannot expect to match the quality of shop-bought fruits. **Citrus mitis** is the most popular species — a 4 ft bush which bears small (1–1½ in. diameter) bitter oranges whilst the plant is still quite small. Other indoor types include the Sweet Orange (**C. sinensis** — 4 ft, spiny, 2½ in. fruits under greenhouse conditions), Lemon (**C. limon** — the dwarf varieties are **meyeri** and the large-fruited **Ponderosa**) and Seville Orange (**C. aurantium** — 3 ft spiny tree).

Skimmia japonica

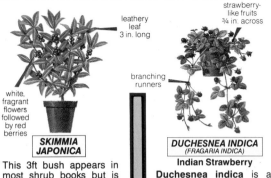

leathery
leaf
3 in. long

strawberry-
like fruits
¾ in. across

branching
runners

white,
fragrant
flowers
followed
by red
berries

SKIMMIA JAPONICA

This 3ft bush appears in most shrub books but is rarely mentioned in house plant guides. Despite its rejection in print, a female specimen in full fruit will provide a colourful display for months in an unheated room. Mist leaves occasionally and plant outdoors after the berries have shrivelled.

DUCHESNEA INDICA
(FRAGARIA INDICA)
Indian Strawberry

Duchesnea indica is a good hanging basket plant which has unfortunately never become popular. The trailing runners bear bright yellow flowers between June and October, and these are followed by the fruits — bright red but tasteless.

Duchesnea indica

---

white, star-shaped
flowers followed
by fruit

oval
leaf
4 in
long

upright
fruits
darkening
with age

CAPSICUM ANNUUM
Christmas Pepper

The Christmas Pepper has long been a favourite for the festive season, each 1 – 1½ ft high shrubby plant bearing numerous brightly-coloured fruits. With proper watering and misting the display will last into the New Year, after which these annual plants are thrown away. There are many varieties, but these are rarely named in the shops. A few bear ball-like fruits, but the popular types bear erect cone-like peppers. These may be 1 in. (**Christmas Greeting**) or 2 in. (**Fiesta**) and the usual pattern is for them to change from green to yellow and finally red. There are variations — some varieties bear purple fruits (**Variegated Flash** is an example) and some are in full colour as early as July — making the common name rather meaningless. These Christmas Peppers have been bred from Chilli Peppers and Cayenne Peppers, so the ornamental fruits are edible . . . but fiery and best avoided.

Capsicum annuum Red Missile

Punica granatum nana

leaf
1 in.
long

red tubular
flowers
followed
by orange
fruit

PUNICA GRANATUM NANA
Dwarf Pomegranate

The Dwarf Pomegranate grows about 3 ft high — an excellent pot plant for a sunny window. The leaves are glossy and bright scarlet flowers appear in summer. Ball-like fruit develop . . . if you are lucky.

oval leaf
4 in. long

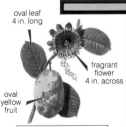

fragrant
flower
4 in. across

oval
yellow
fruit

PASSIFLORA QUADRANGULARIS
Granadilla

A vigorous climber — much larger but rarer than Passiflora caerulea (page 78). This is a plant for the conservatory rather than the living room — under good conditions large fruits appear. A popular tropical fruit, but don't expect much under glass.

Passiflora quadrangularis

CHAPTER 5
FLOWERING HOUSE PLANTS

Flowering house plants are usually (but not always) easier to identify than foliage ones. The best time to identify a mystery plant is when it is in full bloom. Look at the growth habit — the basic division is between the plants which grow upright and the ones with weak stems which either trail or need wires or canes for support. Next, study the blooms carefully — note colour and shape. Size is of course important — you will find the dimensions of the average bloom for each type listed on the following pages. Fragrance is sometimes an important recognition factor — so are plant height, leaf shape and colour, flowering season, and flower arrangement on the stalk. With all of this information you should be able to identify your plant from the diagrams on the following pages.

If you are new to growing house plants, always check the background to a flowering indoor plant after identification. Use a textbook such as The House Plant Expert. This will tell you the plant's likes and dislikes, and it will also tell you the expected life span of the plant. It is vital for you to know whether it is a true house plant which can be kept growing after flowering or if it is a flowering pot plant which will have to be thrown away once the blooms have faded. So many people are disappointed when their gift plant dies after a month or two, never realising that it was not their fault.

Flowering plants are an indispensable part of the indoor plant world — both the temporary ones such as Cinerarias and the permanent types like Geraniums have a vital role to play. The word 'flower' here is used in its widest sense — there are many plants where the true flowers are insignificant, the showy blooms being composed of large and colourful bracts. Amongst the well-known examples are Poinsettia, Aechmea, Vriesea, Anthurium and the Shrimp Plant.

The selection of flowering house plants seems to be largely limited to the range offered in pots by garden centres, florists and High St shops. The favourites include Azalea, Geranium, Busy Lizzie, African Violet, Chrysanthemum, Primula, Poinsettia, Cyclamen, Fuchsia, Cineraria, Kalanchoe and Hydrangea. All are bought when in bud or flower, and these plants dominate the indoor flower scene. All the above plants have earned their place as best-sellers, but this chapter does illustrate just how many fine flowering indoor plants are not in the top twenty. The pattern may be slowly changing — Orchids, Miniature Roses and Bromeliads are appearing in increasing numbers and both Gerberas and Pot Dahlias have now joined the closely-related Pot Chrysanthemum.

Not all flowering house plants need be bought as pot-grown specimens. Some can be grown from seed — catalogues now offer seeds of modern hybrids of Geranium, Cyclamen, Primula, Cineraria, Browallia, Streptocarpus, Calceolaria, etc. All of these types appear in the house plant books, but there is no reason why dwarf varieties of many popular garden annuals should not be raised and grown indoors. Listed on pages 104-105 are a number of annuals which have proved successful as indoor plants.

Bulbs as well as seeds are a neglected source of indoor flowering plants. Of course, millions of Narcissi, Hyacinths, Tulips and Crocuses are planted in bowls each autumn, but the range of bulbs suitable for growing indoors is really much larger. Some are garden bulbs which have a place in the house — others are tender types which need protection from frost. See pages 90-97 for details.

Flowering Climbers & Trailers

A number of flowering plants have either a trailing habit or they climb by twining round or clinging to supports. These are the Climbers & Trailers, but there is really no clear-cut dividing line between this group and the bushy plants with weak stems which soon flop over if not tied to canes. As an example, the Christmas Cactus (page 79) trails gracefully over the rim of the pot and is included here, but many Orchid Cacti (page 103) and Busy Lizzies (page 98) are included in other groups despite the fact that they droop and straggle if not supported. The basic distinction is that true trailers are decorative *because* of their pendent habit and not despite it.

glossy leaf 5 in. long

stems and flower-stalks thin and pendent

flower 1 in. across

BEGONIA GLAUCOPHYLLA
(BEGONIA LIMMINGHEIANA)
Shrimp Begonia

brittle leaf 4 in. across

stems and flower-stalks thin and pendent

flower 2–3 in. across

BEGONIA TUBERHYBRIDA PENDULA
Basket Begonia

Begonia tuberhybrida pendula Bridal Cascade

Pendent begonias are popular plants for hanging baskets, and nearly always a variety of **Begonia tuberhybrida pendula** is chosen for summer flowering. This is the trailing version of the bushy, giant-flowering tuberous begonias which are so well known. Tubers of B. tuberhybrida pendula are planted in spring — the flowers are single or semi-double and you can choose from white, yellow, pink, orange and red. There are **Aphrodite** (pink), **Red Cascade** (red), **Golden Shower** (yellow) and several other varieties to add colour between June and September. For winter flowering **B. glaucophylla** is the type to grow — treat as a trailer or tie to a cane as a climber. The flowers are coral-red.

Pelargonium peltatum roulettii

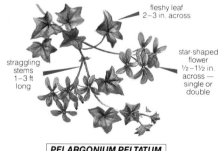

fleshy leaf 2–3 in. across

straggling stems 1–3 ft long

star-shaped flower ½–1½ in. across — single or double

PELARGONIUM PELTATUM
Ivy-leaved Geranium

The Trailing or Ivy-leaved Geranium is widely used in hanging baskets indoors and in bowls on outdoor terraces and patios. The mat-forming drooping stems are brittle and should be handled with care. The summer and autumn flowers are available in a range of colours — **Madame Margot** (white), **Charles Turner** (pink), **Apricot Queen** (salmon), **La France** (lilac) and **Madame Crousse** (red).

Pelargonium peltatum La France

stems 6–12 in. high

leaf 1–1½ in. across — heart-shaped, serrated and velvety

trumpet-like flared flower

ACHIMENES HYBRIDA
Cupid's Bower
(Hot Water Plant)

Achimenes is a weak-stemmed plant — the stems can be left to trail or can be staked to produce a bushy specimen. Height depends on the species. **Achimenes erecta** (a trailer despite its name) produces 18 in. long reddish stems and red blooms — **A. longiflora** is a bigger plant, growing 2 ft high when staked and with 3 in. long leaves. Its flowers are purple. These species are not easy to find — at your local shop you will be offered one of the many types of **A. hybrida**. These compact plants are available in many colours — red, pink, purple, blue, white and yellow, and are much used in hanging baskets. Each bloom is short-lived, but the flowering season lasts from June to October. Named types include **Rose** and **Little Beauty** (pink), **Purple King** and **Paul Arnold** (purple), **Valse Bleu** (blue) and **Ambroise Verschaffelt** (white, veined purple). All Achimenes die down in winter.

Achimenes hybrida English Waltz

Allamanda cathartica grandiflora

tubular flower 3 in. across

leaf 4 in. long

ALLAMANDA CATHARTICA
Golden Trumpet

Truly a beauty, this tall and vigorous climber is not easy to grow outside the conservatory or greenhouse. The flaring trumpets in summer are spectacular — for maximum impact choose **Allamanda cathartica grandiflora** (5 in. wide flowers).

pink or purple flower 1 in. across

leaf narrow and smooth

stems woody and spiny

BOUGAINVILLEA GLABRA
Paper Flower

The showy flowers are really brightly coloured, papery bracts. The basic species is **Bougainvillea glabra**, but its hybrids are more popular. Top of the list is the large-leaved, large-flowered **B. buttiana Mrs Butt** (rose-crimson).

Bougainvillea buttiana Mrs Butt

tubular 2 in. long red flower — brown calyx below, borne at stem tip

leaf 1½ in. long — waxy and edged with purple

stems 1½ ft long

AESCHYNANTHUS LOBBIANUS
Lipstick Vine

The general popular name for Aeschynanthus species is Basket Vine — these plants are excellent for hanging baskets. Unfortunately they are not easy to grow under ordinary room conditions — a feature shared with the closely-related Columnea. The two can be confused — a rough-and-ready way of distinguishing between them is to look at the flower. The upper lobes on the Columnea fuse and form a prominent downturned hood — the lobes of Aeschynanthus form a much less prominent hood. **Aeschynanthus speciosus** is readily available and is also the most colourful — 2–3 ft stems bearing 3 in. long flowers which stand erect, darkening from yellow bases to red mouths. **A. lobbianus** is a smaller plant, its red flowers arising from brown 'lipstick cases' from May to July. **A. hildebrandii** is sold in winter — a small, creeping plant with red flowers. **A. marmoratus** is grown for its foliage (mottled above and red below) rather than the flowers.

Aeschynanthus speciosus

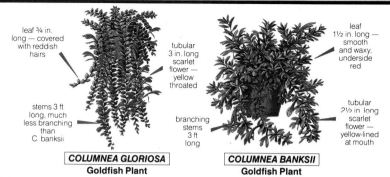

leaf ¾ in. long — covered with reddish hairs

tubular 3 in. long scarlet flower — yellow throated

stems 3 ft long, much less branching than C. banksii

branching stems 3 ft long

leaf 1½ in. long — smooth and waxy, underside red

tubular 2½ in. long scarlet flower — yellow-lined at mouth

COLUMNEA GLORIOSA
Goldfish Plant

COLUMNEA BANKSII
Goldfish Plant

Columnea microphylla

Columneas are superb trailing plants — a cascade of tubular flowers on long, trailing stems. The usual flower colour is red with a yellow throat, but other shades are available for the collector — e.g the golden **Columnea affinis**. If only Columnea was not so difficult — it needs moist air, cool winter nights, careful watering, and so on. Unless you are skilled choose one of the easier ones — the hybrid **C. Stavanger** (3 ft stems, smooth leaves, 3 in. long yellow-throated, red flowers) or **C. banksii**. The hairy-leaved ones are harder to grow. **C. gloriosa** is an old favourite — others include **C. microphylla** (4 ft stems, tiny leaves, small C. gloriosa-like blooms) and **C. hirta** (creeping stems, red flowers in spring).

Campanula isophylla alba

star-shaped flower 1½ in. wide

grey-green hairy stems 1 ft long

CAMPANULA ISOPHYLLA
Italian Bellflower

The popular Campanula is **C. isophylla** (blue). An excellent and easy-to-grow trailer or climber — the varieties **alba** (white) and **mayi** (pale purple) are available. Flowers appear abundantly from midsummer to early autumn. Dead-head to prolong display.

inflated flower 1 in. long — white with red tip

leaf 5 in. long

CLERODENDRUM THOMSONIAE
Glory Bower

Clerodendrum thomsoniae will grow to 8 ft or more if left unpruned — pinch out tips for room display. Allow stems to trail or to twine around an upright support. The leaves have a quilted look and the summer flowers are showy.

Clerodendrum thomsoniae

tubular flower ¾ in. across — orange-red with yellow eye

surface dark green or coppery — veins silver or pale green

leaf 2–4 in. long, covered with rough hairs

tubular flower 1½ in. across — white with feathered edges

surface green and velvety — veins purple or brown

leaf 1–2 in. long, covered with downy hairs

EPISCIA CUPREATA
Flame Violet

EPISCIA DIANTHIFLORA
Lace Flower

Episcia cupreata

Episcia is grown for its attractive foliage and pretty, if rather small, flowers. This trailer requires humid conditions, so it is better to grow it as a ground cover between other plants rather than as an isolated specimen in a pot. It grows by means of runners, which root and produce leaves at intervals, and the two most popular species are shown above. **Episcia cupreata** has produced many hybrids and sports — **Amazon, Metallica, Acajou, Cleopatra** and **Harlequin** are examples. **E. reptans** is not easy to distinguish from some of these varieties — it has the same pale veining (usually pale green against a dark green background) and the surface is heavily wrinkled. On the other hand **E. lilacina** is easy to recognise — the flowers have lilac lobes and a yellow throat.

Dipladenia sanderi rosea

leaf 2 in. long

twining woody stems

trumpet-shaped flower 3 in. across

DIPLADENIA SANDERI ROSEA

A tall climber (up to 10 ft if left unpruned) grown for its glossy leaves and yellow-throated, pink flowers which appear in summer. **Dipladenia (Mandevilla) splendens** is similar, but is larger-leaved with pink-throated flowers.

leaf 1–2 in. long

pendent bell-like flower 1–2 in. long

weak, drooping stems

FUCHSIA HYBRIDA
Lady's Eardrops

There are hundreds of Fuchsia hybrids — most of them grow as compact bushes. A few are Trailing Fuchsias — **Cascade** (white sepals, red petals) is the best known. Others include **Marinka** (red), **Red Ribbons** (white and red) and **Pink Galore** (pink).

Fuchsia hybrida Golden Marinka

Gloriosa superba

leaves bear tendrils at tips

lily-like flower 4 in. long

GLORIOSA ROTHSCHILDIANA
Glory Lily

A spectacular climber reaching 4 ft or more. Swept-back petals of the summer flowers are red with a yellow base — **Gloriosa superba** is similar but petals change from green to orange and finally to red. Gloriosa dies down in winter.

tubular flower ¾ in. long

oval leaf 2 in. long

twining stems

MANETTIA INFLATA
Firecracker Plant

A colourful plant which is unfortunately not easy to find. Leave the stems to trail or train them up canes for a spring to autumn display of flowers. Each bloom is quite small, but they are borne in great profusion.

Manettia inflata

Passiflora caerulea

ornate flower 3 in. across

hand-like leaf 4 in. across

PASSIFLORA CAERULEA
Passion Flower

Passiflora caerulea is a rampant grower, climbing by means of tendrils. Prune hard each spring. It needs cool conditions despite its exotic appearance — the short-lived but showy blooms appear between July and September. Several varieties are available.

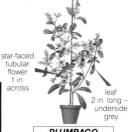

star-faced tubular flower 1 in. across

leaf 2 in. long — underside grey

PLUMBAGO AURICULATA
(PLUMBAGO CAPENSIS)
Cape Leadwort

Grow it as a trailer or tie it to supports as a climber — the stems will reach 3–4 ft. Clusters of sky blue flowers appear throughout the summer and autumn — cut back in spring. A white variety (**alba**) is available.

Plumbago auriculata

fragrant white flower with reddish-purple centre — approximately 10 per cluster

fragrant pale pink flower with red centre — approximately 20 per cluster

non-glossy leaf 1 in. long

glossy leaf .3 in long

HOYA BELLA
Miniature Wax Plant

HOYA CARNOSA VARIEGATA
Golden Wax Plant

Hoya bella

The Wax Plants are climbers or trailers with fleshy leaves and clusters of waxy, star-shaped flowers. The flowering season extends from May to September. **Hoya carnosa** is the basic species — its vigorous twining stems must be trained on wires, trellis or some other form of support. Several varieties are available, including **variegata** (cream-edged leaves), **exotica** (yellow-centred leaves) and **Krimson Princess** (red-coloured young foliage). **H. australis** is quite similar, but its leaves are almost round. **H. bella** is a trailer rather than a climber, and is much more difficult to grow under room conditions than the popular H. carnosa. **H. multiflora** is another species which is commercially available — pale yellow flowers are its claim to fame.

5–7 leaflets per leaf

twining stems

fragrant star-shaped flower 1 in. across

3 leaflets per leaf

non-twining stems

non-fragrant semi-double flower 1–1½ in. across

JASMINUM POLYANTHUM
Pink Jasmine

JASMINUM PRIMULINUM
Primrose Jasmine

Jasminum officinale

Jasmines are grown for the fragrance of their starry white flowers — this applies to the most popular but not to all species. The favourite one is **Jasminum polyanthum**, with pink buds which open between winter and mid spring to produce tubular sweet-smelling flowers. **J. officinale grandiflora** (White Jasmine) is similar in appearance — twining stems, much-divided leaves and long-tubed white and fragrant flowers. There are, however, important differences — the flowers appear in summer or autumn and do not have a rosy tinge on the reverse. Also, the blooms do not appear until the plant is mature. **J. primulinum** (J. mesnyi) is the odd one out — the flowers are yellow with 6 or more petals and fragrance is absent. There are just 3 leaflets per leaf and the stems are not twining — they must be tied to the supports.

flower 1 in. across with 2 tiers of swept-back petals

stems made up of distinctly tooth-edged segments

stems made up of scalloped-edged segments

flower 1½ in. across — open bell of sharply-pointed petals

ZYGOCACTUS TRUNCATUS
(SCHLUMBERGERA TRUNCATA)
Christmas Cactus

RHIPSALIDOPSIS GAERTNERI
(SCHLUMBERGERA GAERTNERI)
Easter Cactus

Rhipsalidopsis gaertneri Electra

Both the popular Christmas and the Easter Cactus have branching and arching stems composed of leaf-like flattened segments which are 1½–2 in. long. The margins are the key to identification — the segments of **Zygocactus truncatus** bear pointed projections whereas those of **Rhipsalidopsis gaertneri** and the smaller **R. rosea** are shallowly scalloped. Plants are usually bought in bud and many varieties are available. Z. truncatus varieties bloom between mid November and late January — white, pink, red or purple. R. gaertneri varieties range from pink to dark red and bloom in April or May. These shop-bought specimens usually produce a large number of blooms, but in unskilled hands never flower again. The reason is that these forest cacti need both a resting period (when water and warmth are decreased) and a spell outdoors in order to produce next year's flower buds.

Abutilon megapotamicum

lantern-like flower 2 in. long

leaf 3 in. long

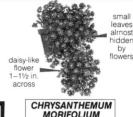

small leaves alrnost hidden by flowers

daisy-like flower 1–1½ in. across

ABUTILON MEGAPOTAMICUM
Trailing Abutilon

A trailing plant for hanging baskets, but tied to supports this evergreen will grow 4 ft high. Between spring and autumn the flowers appear, hanging down from the wiry stems and giving the plant its alternative common name — Weeping Chinese Lantern. The variety **variegata** has yellow-splashed leaves.

CHRYSANTHEMUM MORIFOLIUM
Cascade Chrysanthemum

The bushy Pot Chrysanthemum is one of the most popular plants bought for temporary display. The Cascade varieties of Chrysanthemum are much less well-known and you will have to raise your own from seed. Late summer and autumn flowering — let the stems trail or train into decorative shapes.

Chrysanthemum morifolium The Bride

Saintpaulia Breezy Blue

rounded leaf 2 in. across

violet-like flower 1 in. across

SAINTPAULIA GROTEI
Trailing African Violet

The general growth habit of an African Violet is a flat rosette (see pages 110–111), but trailing types with long stems and alternate leaves can be obtained from specialist nurseries. **Saintpaulia grotei** is the usual ancestor — trailers include **Sky Trailer**, **Snow Trailer**, **Pixie Trail** and **Breezy Blue**.

serrated leaf ½ in. across

4-petalled flower 1 in. across

SCHIZOCENTRON ELEGANS
Spanish Shawl

Use **Schizocentron elegans** as a trailing plant or as ground cover — the dense mat of dark green, small leaves is sprinkled in summer with rose-purple flowers — prominent stamens stand up from the open petals. The creeping reddish stems root at the nodes.

Schizocentron elegans

Stephanotis floribunda

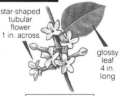

star-shaped tubular flower 1 in. across

glossy leaf 4 in. long

STEPHANOTIS FLORIBUNDA
Wax Flower
(Madagascar Jasmine)

In the conservatory this climbing shrub can reach 10 ft or more — as a house plant it is usually sold with its twining stem laced around a wire hoop. Glossy oval leaves all year round and heavily-scented waxy flowers from May to October make Stephanotis a popular choice.

tubular flower 2 in. across

serrated leaf 2 in. long

THUNBERGIA ALATA
Black-eyed Susan

Quick growing and colourful are the hallmarks of Black-eyed Susan. Sow seeds or buy a plant in spring and a large area can be rapidly covered by its twining stems. Throughout the summer the brown-throated flowers appear, with petals of white, yellow or orange depending upon the variety.

Thunbergia alata

Red Flowers

Most popular genera of flowering house plants, such as Pelargonium, Chrysanthemum and Primula have species and hybrids in a range of colours. The house plant species of a few genera, however, bear blooms which are always red or pink, although there may be a variety or two in other colours. For example, there are white varieties as well as the familiar red or pink ones of Anthurium, Crinum and Vallota. If you can't find your red-flowering plant here, turn to pages 75−80 and 90−118. If it is a succulent or cactus, turn to the appropriate sections.

Acalypha hispida

pendent spike 1½ ft long

hairy leaf 6 in. long

ACALYPHA HISPIDA
Chenille Plant

A tall shrub reaching 6 ft or more, grown for its tassels of tiny red flowers which appear amongst the leaves in late summer and autumn. Not an easy plant to grow indoors — it needs warmth and moist air. **Alba** is an unusual white variety.

Anthurium scherzerianum

waxy 'flower' 2 in. long with curly orange tail

lance-shaped leaf 8 in. long

ANTHURIUM SCHERZERIANUM
Flamingo Flower

glossy, puckered 'flower' 4 in. long with straight or arched yellow tail

heart-shaped leaf 9 in. long

ANTHURIUM ANDREANUM
Oilcloth Flower

Both Anthurium species are expensive and difficult, but few other plants give such an air of luxury. The exotic flower-heads last for 2 months or more — for the technically minded the 'petal' is a spathe and the 'tail' is a spadix. Both need misting at frequent intervals and may need staking — **A. scherzerianum** is more tolerant of ordinary room conditions than the larger **A. andreanum**. Both flower in spring and summer, and nearly all varieties are red.

Callistemon citrinus

erect spike 3 in. long

narrow leaf 3 in. long

CALLISTEMON CITRINUS
Bottlebrush Plant

This silky-stemmed woody plant is not difficult to grow — it will reach about 3 ft high and in summer the cylindrical flower-spikes appear — no petals, just yellow-tipped red stamens. Leaves bronzy when young.

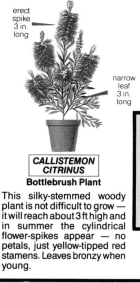

beak-like flower 2 in. long

feathery leaf 6 in. long

CLIANTHUS FORMOSUS
Glory Pea

A rare and short-lived one, growing 2 ft high with feathery leaves and clusters of unusual flowers in late spring or summer. Don't pamper this tropical-looking plant — give it plenty of fresh air in summer.

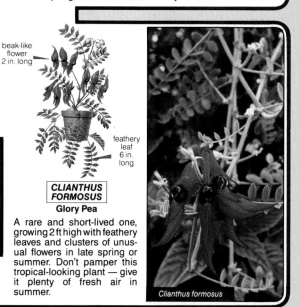

Clianthus formosus

Calliandra inaequilatera

ball-like flower-head 3 in. across

leaflet 2 in. long

CALLIANDRA INAEQUILATERA
Powderpuff Plant

Popular in the U.S. but rare in Britain, this tree bears 'powder puffs' composed entirely of stamens. It should be kept pruned to 2–3 ft. The flower-heads last for 6–8 weeks — a winter bloomer which should be better known.

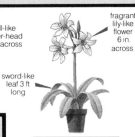

fragrant lily-like flower 6 in. across

sword-like leaf 3 ft long

CRINUM POWELLII
Swamp Lily

Everything about **Crinum powellii** is extraordinarily large — the 6 in. bulbs, the 3 ft tall flower-stalks and the magnificent 7 in. long trumpets which appear in late summer. Hybrids in white and red as well as pink are available.

Crinum powellii

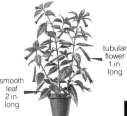

tubular flower 1 in. long

smooth leaf 2 in. long

CUPHEA IGNEA
Cigar Plant

Unspectacular, but pleasant enough when grouped with other plants. The neat 1 ft high bush produces flowers from April to November — red tubes with white and purple mouths. With a little imagination — a tiny cigar with ash at the tip.

yellow-centred 'flower' ½ in. across

narrow leaf 4 in. long

EUPHORBIA FULGENS
Scarlet Plume

The well-known Crown of Thorns is described on page 62 — Scarlet Plume is a much less popular Euphorbia. This 4 ft tree bears smooth arching stems which are studded with scarlet 'flowers' (bright bracts surrounding true flowers) during the winter months.

Euphorbia fulgens

Cuphea ignea

ball-like flower-head 8 in. across

wavy leaf 1 ft long

HAEMANTHUS KATHARINAE
Blood Lily

A 1 ft flower-stalk appears from the base of this bulbous plant in summer — this is crowned by a globular collection of tubular red flowers. The flower-head of **H. multiflorus** is smaller and appears earlier.

Haemanthus katharinae

plume-like flower-head 5 in. long

coarse leaf 6 in. long

JACOBINIA CARNEA
King's Crown

J. carnea flowers in late summer, each pink pompon bearing numerous 2 in. tubular flowers. Old plants are unattractive — replace the 3 ft high bushes after 2 years. **J. pauciflora** bears yellow-tipped scarlet flowers in winter.

Jacobinia carnea

Jatropha podagrica

lobed leaf 1 ft across

flower-head 2 in. across

JATROPHA PODAGRICA

This peculiar plant grows about 2 ft tall — a conversation piece rather than a thing of beauty. In late winter the flower-stalks with a crown of small red blooms grow from the swollen brown stem. Leaves appear later.

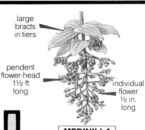

large bracts in tiers

pendent flower-head 1½ ft long

individual flower ½ in. long

MEDINILLA MAGNIFICA
Rose Grape

The pride of any collection, but almost certainly not for you. It requires a warm greenhouse or a special plant window plus skill and care. A 5 ft shrub with 9 in. oval leaves, and in late spring the superb flower-heads.

Medinilla magnifica

velvety leaf 4 in. long

tubular flower 2 in. long

RECHSTEINERIA CARDINALIS
(GESNERIA CARDINALIS)
Cardinal Flower

A bright summer-flowering plant closely related to Gloxinia — see page 100. The hooded, bright red blooms are borne horizontally at the top of the 1 ft stems. **R. leucotricha** (Brazilian Edelweiss) has woolly silvery-grey leaves.

Rechsteineria cardinalis

trumpet-shaped flower 1½ in. across

oval leaf 3 in. long

purple underside

RUELLIA MAKOYANA
Monkey Plant

R. makoyana is a low-growing plant cultivated for its decorative foliage (silver-veined olive green) and winter flowers. The weak stems can be left to trail — pinch out tips to induce bushiness. **R. macrantha** is a much bigger plant.

Ruellia macrantha

Sprekelia formosissima

upper 3 petals curled backwards

prominent stamens

lower 3 petals form short tube

SPREKELIA FORMOSISSIMA
Jacobean Lily

A bulbous plant which produces a 1½ ft flower-stalk crowned with a large red flower in summer. The long, strap-like leaves appear when flowering is finished. The bloom has a unique shape, as shown above.

bell-like flower 3 in. across

sword-like leaf 1 ft long

VALLOTA SPECIOSA
Scarborough Lily

An excellent plant for a sunny windowsill — the leaves are evergreen and in late summer scarlet trumpets open at the crown of the 1–2 ft flower-stalks. White and salmon varieties are available, but are rarely seen.

Vallota speciosa

Blue Flowers

Most popular genera of flowering house plants, such as Pelargonium, Chrysanthemum and Primula have species and hybrids in a range of colours. The house plant species of a few genera, however, bear blooms which are always blue or purple, although there may be a variety or two in other colours. For example, there are white varieties of Agapanthus, Browallia and Heliotropium. If you can't find your blue-flowering plant here, turn to pages 75—80 and 90—118. If it is a succulent or cactus, turn to the appropriate section.

Agapanthus orientalis

ball-like flower-head 3–8 in. across

strap-like leaf 1 ft long

AGAPANTHUS AFRICANUS
Blue African Lily

Long tubular flowers are borne in a spherical cluster on top of the 2 ft flower-stalks which appear in succession throughout the summer. Plant in a tub or large pot — **A. orientalis** is larger and will need even more space.

Browallia major

star-shaped tubular flower 2 in. across

drooping leaf 2 in. long

BROWALLIA SPECIOSA
Bush Violet

Blue flowers with white throats, borne in profusion during autumn on the weak stems — stake to maintain bushy shape. Buy in flower or grow from seed. Varieties **major** (large blue flowers) and **alba** (white flowers) are available.

fragrant, white-eyed flower 2 in. across

leathery leaf 3 in. long

BRUNFELSIA CALYCINA
Yesterday, Today and Tomorrow

Clusters of flowers appear on this 1–2 ft evergreen. The unusual common name describes the changing colours — violet yesterday, blue today and white tomorrow. The blooms are borne nearly all year round, with just a short winter break.

Brunfelsia calycina

Eranthemum nervosum

purple-eyed flower 1 in. across

rough leaf 3 in. long

ERANTHEMUM NERVOSUM
Blue Sage

A shrubby plant (1½–2 ft tall) which blooms in winter. The flowers appear between the green bracts which cover the spike-like flower-head. **E. wattii** is a smaller plant with purple flowers. Neither is easy to find.

fragrant gold-centred flower ½ in. across

shiny leaf 1 in. long

EXACUM AFFINE
Arabian Violet

Raise from seed or buy this plant when the first flower buds are beginning to open. The floral display lasts for several months — prolong it by regularly removing dead flowers. Treat as an annual — throw away once the flowering season is over.

Exacum affine Starlight Fragrance

Felicia amelloides

daisy-like flower 1 in. across

oval leaf ½ in. long

fragrant flower-head 4–6 in. across

deeply-veined leaf 3 in. long

FELICIA AMELLOIDES
Blue Daisy

A rare shrubby plant, growing about 1 ft tall and bearing sky blue daisies with prominent yellow centres almost all year round. Midsummer is the main flowering period — the blooms on their wiry stems open only in sunlight.

HELIOTROPIUM HYBRIDUM
Heliotrope

An excellent but little-used shrub for indoor decoration — the large heads of tiny flowers will perfume a room from May until October. The usual colour is purple, but blue and white varieties are available.

Heliotropium hybridum Mrs Lowther

Liriope muscari

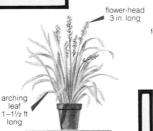

flower-head 3 in. long

arching leaf 1–1½ ft long

foxglove-like flower ¾ in. across

leathery leaf 4 in. long

LIRIOPE MUSCARI
Blue Lily Turf

The 1 ft tall flowering spike looks rather like a giant Grape Hyacinth — the ¼ in. violet ball-like flowers cluster around the tip from August to October. The leathery grassy leaves are evergreen. White-flowered and striped-leaved varieties are available.

TETRANEMA MEXICANUM
Mexican Foxglove

A pretty miniature which you will have to raise from seed. In summer the 6 in. flower-stalks arise from the rosette of dark leaves, each stalk bearing a small cluster of pendent violet flowers. Best in partial shade.

Tetranema mexicanum

Tibouchina semidecandra

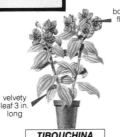

bowl-shaped flower 3 in. across

velvety leaf 3 in. long

tubular flower 1 in. across

serrated leaf 2 in. long

TIBOUCHINA SEMIDECANDRA
Glory Bush

You will not find **T. semi-decandra** (**T. urvilleana**) at your local garden centre, so you will have to raise this 4 ft shrub from seed. Between July and November the flowers appear — silky purple with prominent stamens.

TORENIA FOURNIERI
Wishbone Flower

A summer-flowering annual grown from seed — the tips of the stems bear flowers which are quite unmistakable. The face of each bloom is violet with a dark purple lower lip and a distinctive yellow blotch.

Torenia fournieri

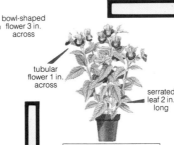

White Flowers

Most popular genera of flowering house plants, such as Pelargonium, Chrysanthemum and Primula have species and hybrids in a range of colours. The house plant species of a few genera, however, bear blooms which are always white, ivory or cream, although there may be a variety or two in other colours. For example, there are yellow Daturas and pink Myrtles. If you can't find your white-flowering plant here, turn to pages 75–80 and 90–118. If it is a succulent or cactus, turn to the appropriate sections.

Datura suaveolens

oval leaf 9 in. long

tubular flower 8–10 in. long

DATURA CANDIDA
Angel's Trumpet

Two species are occasionally sold as house plants — **D. candida** and **D. suaveolens**. Both bear pendulous, sweet-smelling bells — pure white and breathtakingly large. Before rushing off to buy one, however, remember that they need space, care, and all parts are poisonous.

Eucharis grandiflora

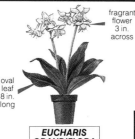

fragrant flower 3 in. across

oval leaf 8 in. long

EUCHARIS GRANDIFLORA
Amazon Lily

E. grandiflora flowers in late winter and may bloom again in summer. This bulbous plant bears clusters of white flowers on top of 2 ft stalks. Each bloom looks like a daffodil with a spiky trumpet.

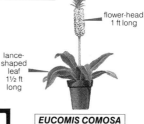

flower-head 1 ft long

lance-shaped leaf 1½ ft long

EUCOMIS COMOSA
Pineapple Lily

E. comosa is a summer-flowering bulbous plant which needs lots of space. The long leaves form a large rosette and the cylindrical spike of small flowers bears a leafy crown. **E. bicolor** (purplish-green flowers, purple-spotted stalk) is smaller.

Eucomis comosa

Gardenia jasminoides

fragrant flower 3 in. across

glossy leaf 4 in. long

GARDENIA JASMINOIDES
Gardenia

A delightful but temperamental shrub — attractive dark green leaves all year round and, when conditions are right, summer flowers which fill the air with fragrance. These blooms are semi-double or double with waxy petals.

fragrant flower ¾ in. across

oval leaf 2 in. long

MYRTUS COMMUNIS
Myrtle

Fragrant flowers, evergreen foliage and easy to grow — yet Myrtle is not popular as a house plant. The bowl-shaped blooms have a prominent central boss of golden stamens. Where space is limited choose the variety **microphylla**.

Myrtus communis

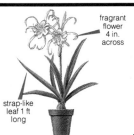

fragrant flower 4 in. across

strap-like leaf 1 ft long

HYMENOCALLIS FESTALIS
Spider Lily

A bulbous plant with attractive sweet-smelling blooms which appear in late spring or summer. These flowers look like daffodils with long and narrow petals, borne on 2 ft stalks above the arching leaves. The foliage of **H. festalis** dies down in winter.

Hymenocallis festalis

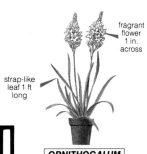

fragrant flower 1 in. across

strap-like leaf 1 ft long

ORNITHOGALUM THYRSOIDES
Chincherinchee

Strap-like leaves arise from the bulb, followed by a 1½ ft stalk crowned with about 20 starry flowers in late spring. A close relative (**O. caudatum**) has a 3 ft stalk which bears up to 100 green-striped blooms.

Ornithogalum thyrsoides

fragrant flower ½ in. across

leathery leaf 4 in. long

PITTOSPORUM TOBIRA
Mock Orange

A flat-topped tree with dark glossy leaves — in spring the branches are topped with clusters of tubular star-faced flowers. The colour is creamy-white and the fragrance is reminiscent of orange blossom. Very easy to grow.

Pittosporum tobira

fragrant flower 1 in. across

grass-like leaf 1 ft long

POLIANTHES TUBEROSA
Tuberose

The Tuberose, so widely planted in the Tropics, is not often grown in Europe. The bulb-like tubers are planted in spring in order to bloom in winter. The leaves are strap shaped, and the flowering spike grows 2–3 ft tall.

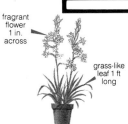

Polianthes tuberosa

golden-centred flower 1½ in. across

downy leaf 9 in. long

SPARMANNIA AFRICANA
House Lime

The House Lime is tree-like, quickly reaching several feet high. The leaves are soft and pale, and the flowers appear in long-stalked clusters in early spring. Prune after blooming has finished — repeat flowering may occur.

Sparmannia africana

arum-like flower 3 in. long

lance-shaped leaf 6 in. long

SPATHIPHYLLUM WALLISII
Peace Lily

Long-stalked glossy leaves grow directly out of the compost and in late spring the long-lasting flowers appear. The so-called flower is really a white spathe with a yellow spadix. **S. wallisii** grows about 1 ft high — **S. Mauna Loa** is larger.

Spathiphyllum wallisii

Yellow Flowers

Most popular genera of flowering house plants, such as Pelargonium, Chrysanthemum and Primula have species and hybrids in a range of colours. The house plant species of a few genera, however, bear blooms which are always yellow or orange, although there may be a variety or two in other colours. For example, there are red Aphelandras. If you can't find your yellow-flowering plant here, turn to pages 75—80 and 90—118. If it is a succulent or cactus, turn to the appropriate sections.

Acacia dealbata

spiny leaf 1 in. long

ball-like flower-head ½ in. across

ACACIA ARMATA
Kangaroo Thorn

Acacias are useful shrubs where space is not a problem, but they have never been popular. **A. armata** is the best known, reaching 3—4 ft and covered with dark green 'leaves' (really modified leaf stalks). The fluffy flower-heads appear in spring. The ferny-leaved **A. dealbata** is more attractive but much larger.

Aphelandra squarrosa louisae

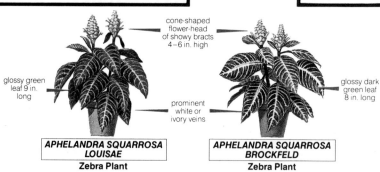

cone-shaped flower-head of showy bracts 4—6 in. high

glossy green leaf 9 in. long

prominent white or ivory veins

glossy dark green leaf 8 in. long

APHELANDRA SQUARROSA LOUISAE
Zebra Plant

APHELANDRA SQUARROSA BROCKFELD
Zebra Plant

The Zebra Plant has been a favourite for generations. All year round its large leaves with silvery veins provide an attractive feature, and then for about 6 weeks in autumn it is crowned by a golden cone. This is made up of bracts which are nearly always yellow or golden, but there is a scarlet type — **A. aurantica**. The most popular Zebra Plant is **A. squarrosa** and the common variety is the golden **louisae** (1—1½ ft). Other varieties are the compact **Dania** and **Brockfeld** — **Fritz Prinsler** is grown for its stunning leaves.

Calathea crocata

globular flower-head 2 in. across

leathery leaf 7 in. long

CALATHEA CROCATA

Calatheas are grown for their unusual foliage (see pages 45 and 50), but not this one. **C. crocata** is a flowering plant which has appeared in garden centres before appearing in the textbooks. Thus its round heads of orange bracts make a display which few people can recognise.

ragged-petalled flower 2 in. across

glossy leaf 5 in. long

COSTUS IGNEUS
Spiral Ginger

A rarity, but well worth looking for. This tropical beauty grows only about 1½ ft tall, the tapered leaves spiralling around the reddish stem. The flowers open in spring — brightly-coloured but unfortunately short-lived. **C. speciosus** is much larger.

Costus igneus

Crossandra undulifolia

tubular flower, 1½ in. across

glossy leaf 3 in. long

CROSSANDRA UNDULIFOLIA
Firecracker Flower

C. undulifolia (C. infundibuliformis) is a good choice — the shiny, wavy-edged leaves are attractive and the orange flowers are borne on 4 in. high green spikes from spring to autumn. Unfortunately, this 1–2 ft shrub will fail if the air is dry.

pea-like flower ¾ in. long

silky leaflet ½ in. long

CYTISUS RACEMOSUS
Genista

Cytisus outdoors is called Broom — indoors it is Genista. Long sprays of fragrant yellow flowers appear in spring at the end of arching branches. The leaves are 3-lobed and there are 2 species — choose **C. racemosus** rather than **C. canariensis.**

Cytisus racemosus

pouch-like flower 1 in. long

glossy leaf 1½ in. long

Hypocyrta glabra

HYPOCYRTA GLABRA
Clog Plant

H. glabra needs moist air and so is not often seen. The branches are erect or gracefully arching, the leaves are dark green and fleshy, and the orange blooms (June–July) are waxy. **H. nummularia** is a trailing relative.

golden flower-head 5 in. long

oval leaf 4 in. long

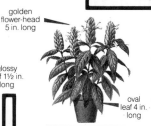

PACHYSTACHYS LUTEA
Lollipop Plant

A newcomer to the house plant scene, but already a popular plant. Shrubby — 1½–2 ft high, with a flower-head made up of golden bracts with white blooms peeping through. Flowering begins in spring and lasts for several months.

Pachystachys lutea

tubular flower 2 in. long

prominently-veined leaf 1 ft long

Sanchezia nobilis

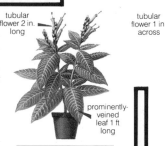

SANCHEZIA NOBILIS

S. nobilis (S. speciosa) is a larger but much less popular relative of the Zebra Plant (page 88). The 3ft bush bears large leaves with white or yellow veins, and the flowers appear in clusters of 8–12 in early summer.

tubular flower 1 in. across

wrinkled leaf 2 in. long

STREPTOSOLEN JAMESONII
Marmalade Bush

You won't find it at your local shop — the Marmalade Bush will have to be searched for. Its main feature is the large cluster of marmalade-coloured flowers borne at the tip of each branch in summer.

Streptosolen jamesonii

Multicoloured Flowers

Most of our well-known flowering house plants are available in a wide range of colours. Varieties of Freesias, Miniature Roses, Primulas, Lilies, Epiphyllums, etc can be obtained in most colours. Others, such as Cyclamen, Azalea and Gloxinia have a somewhat more limited range but the varieties still span part of the rainbow.

or

Thus many of the house plant species we grow have varieties in various hues and these are included in this section. Also included are plants in which the flower itself is multicoloured — the yellow and red Lachenalia, Smithiantha, Calceolaria, Beloperone and so on. Here you will find the many-hued Schizanthus, Fuchsia and Orchid. The photographs and drawings provide a kaleidoscope of colour, to inspire you to widen the range of the plants you buy or raise from seed and bulbs.

● INDOOR BULBS

The word *bulb* in the heading of this section has no botanical significance — it really refers to *bulbous plants.* This group includes all plants which produce fleshy underground organs and which can be bought in this dormant state as planting material. Included here are the true bulbs, corms, tubers and some rhizomes — for definitions of these terms see pages 120-121.

These bulbous plants are truly a mixed bag with no family similarities, and are dealt with in various sections of this book. First of all, there are the **Single-colour Bulbs** (pages 82-87) — here you will find Crinum, Eucharis, Eucomis, Haemanthus, Hymenocallis, Sprekelia, Ornithogalum, Polianthes and Vallota. There are also **Climbers** — Achimenes (page 76) and Gloriosa (page 78). Some bulbs are widely grown indoors but are generally regarded as popular **Garden Bulbs** (pages 94-97) — here you will find the Tulips, Hyacinths, Daffodils, Bluebells etc. A few, such as the tuberous Begonia, Oxalis, Lily, Cyclamen and Dahlia, are dealt with as ordinary multicoloured flowers and appear later in this chapter. Many bulbous plants still remain — these are the non-climbing types which are available in various colours, and they are described in this section.

Hippeastrum Safari

Hippeastrum Apple Blossom

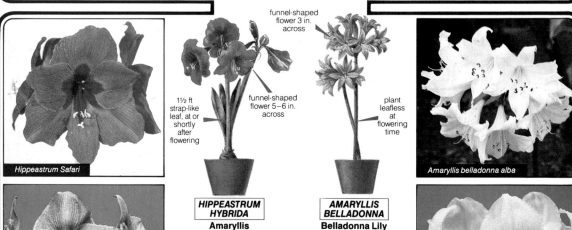

funnel-shaped flower 3 in. across

1½ ft strap-like leaf, at or shortly after flowering

funnel-shaped flower 5–6 in. across

plant leafless at flowering time

HIPPEASTRUM HYBRIDA	**AMARYLLIS BELLADONNA**
Amaryllis	**Belladonna Lily**

These 2 plants are often confused — both are large bulbs which produce clusters of trumpet-like flowers on thick stalks. The Belladonna Lily, however, is not often seen — the popular 'Amaryllis' offered for sale in autumn is really a Hippeastrum hybrid. These hybrids are orange, purple, white, pink or red — sometimes edged or striped in other shades. **H. hybrida** has hollow stalks and there are 3–6 flowers per cluster. **A. belladonna** has solid stalks and 6-12 flowers per cluster. Hippeastrum blooms in winter or spring (Amaryllis — autumn).

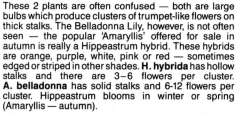

Amaryllis belladonna alba

Hippeastrum Ludwig's Dazzler

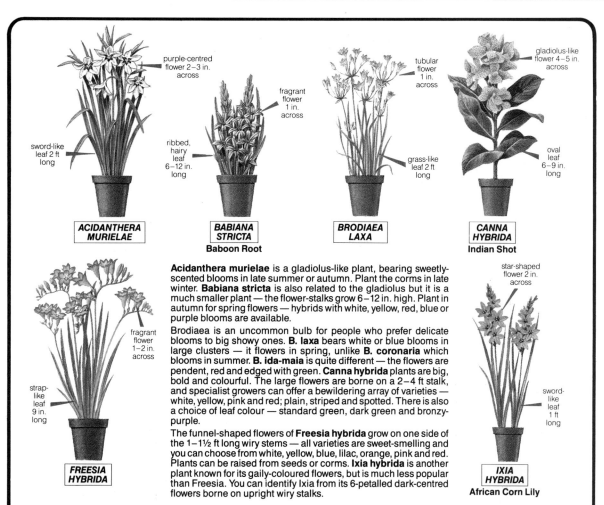

ACIDANTHERA MURIELAE

purple-centred flower 2–3 in. across

sword-like leaf 2 ft long

BABIANA STRICTA

Baboon Root

fragrant flower 1 in. across

ribbed, hairy leaf 6–12 in. long

BRODIAEA LAXA

tubular flower 1 in. across

grass-like leaf 2 ft long

CANNA HYBRIDA

Indian Shot

gladiolus-like flower 4–5 in. across

oval leaf 6–9 in. long

FREESIA HYBRIDA

fragrant flower 1–2 in. across

strap-like leaf 9 in. long

IXIA HYBRIDA

African Corn Lily

star-shaped flower 2 in. across

sword-like leaf 1 ft long

Acidanthera murielae is a gladiolus-like plant, bearing sweetly-scented blooms in late summer or autumn. Plant the corms in late winter. **Babiana stricta** is also related to the gladiolus but it is a much smaller plant — the flower-stalks grow 6–12 in. high. Plant in autumn for spring flowers — hybrids with white, yellow, red, blue or purple blooms are available.

Brodiaea is an uncommon bulb for people who prefer delicate blooms to big showy ones. **B. laxa** bears white or blue blooms in large clusters — it flowers in spring, unlike **B. coronaria** which blooms in summer. **B. ida-maia** is quite different — the flowers are pendent, red and edged with green. **Canna hybrida** plants are big, bold and colourful. The large flowers are borne on a 2–4 ft stalk, and specialist growers can offer a bewildering array of varieties — white, yellow, pink and red; plain, striped and spotted. There is also a choice of leaf colour — standard green, dark green and bronzy-purple.

The funnel-shaped flowers of **Freesia hybrida** grow on one side of the 1–1½ ft long wiry stems — all varieties are sweet-smelling and you can choose from white, yellow, blue, lilac, orange, pink and red. Plants can be raised from seeds or corms. **Ixia hybrida** is another plant known for its gaily-coloured flowers, but is much less popular than Freesia. You can identify Ixia from its 6-petalled dark-centred flowers borne on upright wiry stalks.

Acidanthera murielae

Canna hybrida J B van der Schoot

Freesia hybrida Marie Louise

● INDOOR BULBS continued

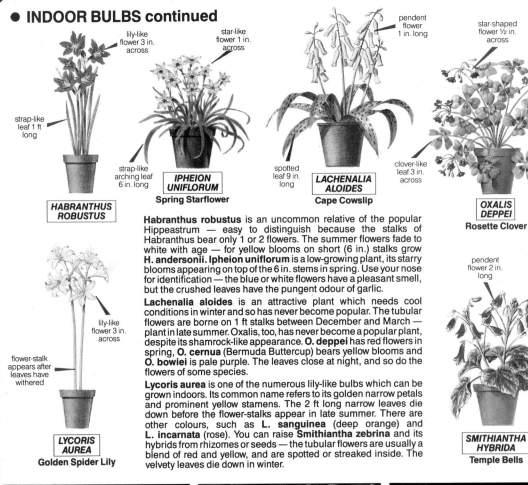

lily-like
flower 3 in.
across

star-like
flower 1 in.
across

pendent
flower
1 in. long

star-shaped
flower ½ in.
across

strap-like
leaf 1 ft
long

strap-like
arching leaf
6 in. long

**IPHEION
UNIFLORUM**
Spring Starflower

spotted
leaf 9 in.
long

**LACHENALIA
ALOIDES**
Cape Cowslip

clover-like
leaf 3 in.
across

**OXALIS
DEPPEI**
Rosette Clover

**HABRANTHUS
ROBUSTUS**

lily-like
flower 3 in.
across

flower-stalk
appears after
leaves have
withered

**LYCORIS
AUREA**
Golden Spider Lily

pendent
flower 2 in.
long

**SMITHIANTHA
HYBRIDA**
Temple Bells

mottled
leaf 4 in.
long

Habranthus robustus is an uncommon relative of the popular Hippeastrum — easy to distinguish because the stalks of Habranthus bear only 1 or 2 flowers. The summer flowers fade to white with age — for yellow blooms on short (6 in.) stalks grow **H. andersonii. Ipheion uniflorum** is a low-growing plant, its starry blooms appearing on top of the 6 in. stems in spring. Use your nose for identification — the blue or white flowers have a pleasant smell, but the crushed leaves have the pungent odour of garlic.

Lachenalia aloides is an attractive plant which needs cool conditions in winter and so has never become popular. The tubular flowers are borne on 1 ft stalks between December and March — plant in late summer. Oxalis, too, has never become a popular plant, despite its shamrock-like appearance. **O. deppei** has red flowers in spring, **O. cernua** (Bermuda Buttercup) bears yellow blooms and **O. bowiei** is pale purple. The leaves close at night, and so do the flowers of some species.

Lycoris aurea is one of the numerous lily-like bulbs which can be grown indoors. Its common name refers to its golden narrow petals and prominent yellow stamens. The 2 ft long narrow leaves die down before the flower-stalks appear in late summer. There are other colours, such as **L. sanguinea** (deep orange) and **L. incarnata** (rose). You can raise **Smithiantha zebrina** and its hybrids from rhizomes or seeds — the tubular flowers are usually a blend of red and yellow, and are spotted or streaked inside. The velvety leaves die down in winter.

Ipheion uniflorum Wisley Blue

Lachenalia aloides

Smithiantha hybrida Cathedral

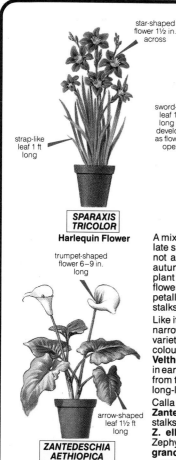

star-shaped flower 1½ in. across

strap-like leaf 1 ft long

SPARAXIS TRICOLOR

Harlequin Flower

lily-like flower 3 in. across

sword-like leaf 1 ft long — develops as flowers open

NERINE FLEXUOSA

saucer-shaped flower 2 in. across

strap-like leaf 1 ft long

TRITONIA CROCATA

Blazing Star

flower-head 4 in. tall

wavy-edged leaf 1 ft long

VELTHEIMIA CAPENSIS

Forest Lily

trumpet-shaped flower 6–9 in. long

arrow-shaped leaf 1½ ft long

ZANTEDESCHIA AETHIOPICA

Calla Lily

crocus-like flower 3 in. across

strap-like leaf 5 in. long

ZEPHYRANTHES GRANDIFLORA

Zephyr Lily

A mixture of hybrids of **Sparaxis tricolor** will produce a riot of colour in late spring when the flowers open above the dense foliage. Many (but not all) types have a black-edged yellow throat. Plant the corms in autumn — leaves die down in winter. **Nerine flexuosa** is an uncommon plant — a cluster of wavy-petalled pink or white bells are borne on 2 ft flower-stalks in autumn. **N. sarniensis** is the Guernsey Lily — narrow-petalled white, orange or red flowers tightly clustered crowning the stalks. The leaves appear after flowering.

Like its relatives Ixia and Sparaxis, **Tritonia crocata** produces a fan of narrow leaves. In summer the floral display appears on wiry stalks — varieties in white, glowing orange, deep pink and several other bright colours are available. Somewhat like the Red Hot Poker of the garden, **Veltheimia capensis** is a good choice for indoors. Plant the large bulb in early autumn and about 3 or 4 months later the 1 ft flower-stalk arises from the centre of the leaf rosette. This stalk bears about 60 small but long-lasting bell-like flowers.

Calla Lily is one of the real beauties of the indoor plant world. **Zantedeschia aethiopica** bears its upturned white trumpets on 3 ft stalks in early spring — other species include **Z. rehmannii** (pink) and **Z. elliottiana** (yellow), plus many hybrids in various colours. The Zephyr Lily is a much smaller and more dainty plant — **Zephyranthes grandiflora** produces 6 in. flower-stalks in early summer, each bearing a crocus-like bloom which soon opens out into a pink star. **Z. candida** (white) is even smaller, but there are several large-flowering hybrids.

Veltheimia capensis

Zantedeschia aethiopica

Zephyranthes grandiflora

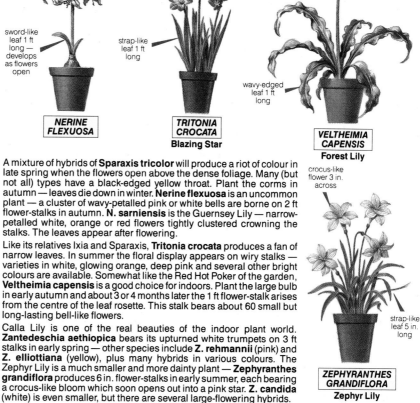

● GARDEN BULBS

Many of the popular bulbs which grace the outdoor spring garden are also planted indoors to provide flowers at the start of the year in the living room. With large bulbs the usual routine is to 'force' specimens which will bloom well ahead of their garden counterparts — this involves keeping the pots or bowls in the cold and dark during root development and then providing more heat and light to stimulate leaf and flower development. Bulbs will not provide a second display indoors — store them and then plant out in the garden in autumn.

Choose with care — not all outdoor varieties are suitable for indoor cultivation, and choose with some spirit of adventure — there really is more than tulips, daffodils, hyacinths and crocuses to pick from!

The most satisfactory Tulips to grow indoors are the compact hybrids classed as Single Earlies (one ring of petals) and Double Earlies (several rings of petals). Some Species Tulips are also excellent for indoor use — both **T. kaufmanniana** and **T. greigii** include suitable varieties. The tall-growing tulips which are so colourful outdoors in May are much less useful for growing in bowls or pots. The best ones to choose are the strong-stemmed Darwin and Lily-flowered hybrids, but even here some form of support will be necessary for the flower-stalks.

Plant: September-October (early September for bulbs prepared for Xmas flowering)

In flower: January-April

TULIPA HYBRIDA Single Early Tulip	**TULIPA HYBRIDA** Double Early Tulip	**TULIPA HYBRIDA** Darwin Tulip	**TULIPA HYBRIDA** Lily-flowered Tulip	**TULIPA KAUFMANNIANA** Species Tulip	**TULIPA GREIGII** Species Tulip
9–16 in. tall Blooms rather small — open flat when mature. Examples: **Brilliant Star** (red) **Bellona** (yellow) **Princess Margaret** (pink) **Keizerskroon** (yellow and red)	9–16 in. tall Long-lasting — petals sometimes frilled. Examples: **Peach Blossom** (rosy-pink) **Orange Nassau** (orange) **Scarlet Cardinal** (red) **Murillo** (pink and white)	24–30 in. tall Very large flowers opening in April. Examples: **Apeldoorn** (red) **Striped Apeldoorn** (yellow and red) **Sunkist** (gold) **Bartigon** (red)	20–24 in. tall Long flowers with pointed reflexed petals. Examples: **West Point** (yellow) **China Pink** (pink) **Aladdin** (red and yellow) **Queen of Sheba** (orange and red)	6–10 in. tall The Water Lily Tulip — the pointed petals opening flat in sunlight. Examples: **The First** (white and red) **Stresa** (red and yellow) **Gluck** (red and yellow)	8–12 in. tall Later than T. kaufmanniana — leaves are streaked or mottled with brown. Examples: **Red Riding Hood** (red) **Oriental Splendour** (yellow and red) **Plaisir** (cream and red)

Tulipa Brilliant Star

Tulipa Peach Blossom

Tulipa greigii Plaisir

Pots of Narcissi and Daffodils continue to be the heralds of spring in countless households. Nearly all types can be grown indoors, but the 5 groups described below are generally considered to be the most reliable. The name 'Daffodil' is used when the large central tube ('trumpet') is at least as long as one of the petals — all the rest of the plants are called Narcissi. Some of the large-flowered types are quite suitable for indoor cultivation, but perhaps the best group of all are the Tazettas which produce bunches of flowers on each stem at Christmas or early in the New Year.

Plant: August-October

In flower: January-April (Tazettas: December-January)

NARCISSUS HYBRIDA	NARCISSUS HYBRIDA	NARCISSUS HYBRIDA	NARCISSUS CYCLAMINEUS	NARCISSUS TAZETTA
Daffodil	**Single Narcissus**	**Double Narcissus**	**Cyclamineus Narcissus**	**Tazetta Narcissus**
12–20 in. tall One flower per stem — central trumpet surrounded by shorter petals.	12–24 in. tall One flower per stem — central cup surrounded by longer petals.	12–18 in. tall More than one ring of petals — cup and petals indistinguishable.	6–12 in. tall Drooping flowers with long trumpets and strongly reflexed petals.	12–18 in. tall Several flowers per stem — central cup surrounded by longer petals.
Examples:	Examples:	Examples:	Examples:	Examples:
King Alfred (yellow)	**Carlton** (yellow)	**White Lion** (white and yellow)	**Peeping Tom** (yellow)	**Soleil d'Or** (yellow)
Spellbinder (white and yellow)	**Verona** (white)	**Golden Ducat** (yellow)	**Tête-a-Tête** (yellow)	**Paperwhite** (white)
Mount Hood (creamy white)	**La Riante** (white and orange)	**Texas** (yellow and orange)	**February Gold** (yellow)	**Geranium** (white and orange)
Dutch Master (yellow)	**Passionale** (white and pink)	**Irene Copeland** (white and yellow)	**Dove Wings** (cream and yellow)	**Cragford** (white and orange)

Narcissus Dutch Master

Narcissus Golden Ducat

Narcissus Paperwhite

Crocus chrysanthus Cream Beauty

flower 3–4 in. long

flower 4–5 in. long

CROCUS CHRYSANTHUS	CROCUS VERNUS
Crocus	**Crocus**

Crocus corms are planted in autumn for flowering in early spring. The varieties of **C. chrysanthus** are often yellow (**Cream Beauty, E. A. Bowles, Goldilocks**, etc), but pale blues and mauves also occur, often with a golden base — **Blue Pearl, Princess Beatrix,** and so on. Flowering time is January-February — the varieties of **C. vernus** bloom a few weeks later, the flowers are larger, and blues and whites predominate. Popular types include **Vanguard** (silvery-lilac), **Kathleen Parlow** (white) and **Pickwick** (mauve, striped purple).

Crocus vernus Vanguard

Multicoloured Flowers

● GARDEN BULBS continued

Iris reticulata

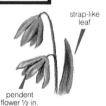

flower 3 in. across

flower-stalk 6 in. long

IRIS RETICULATA

flower-stalk 4 in. long

IRIS DANFORDIAE

Iris danfordiae

Dwarf Irises are excellent for growing indoors, producing large blooms in January and February. They have never gained the popularity of crocuses, hyacinths, etc, but there are at least 3 species which are well worth cultivating in the house. Plant the bulbs in September and provide plenty of light once the leaves have appeared above the compost. Choose from **Iris histrioides major** (deep blue, white centres), **I. reticulata** (purple, yellow centres — fragrant) and **I. danfordiae** (yellow — fragrant).

Scilla tubergeniana

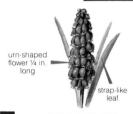

strap-like leaf

pendent flower ½ in. long

SCILLA SIBERICA
Bluebell

Some garden species can be grown indoors — plant in September-October for blooming in January-March. **S. tubergeniana** (3 in.) is the earliest species — **S. siberica** (6 in.) is the popular one. There are tender types (**S. adlamii, S. violacea**) which can be kept indoors for years.

urn-shaped flower ¼ in. long

strap-like leaf

MUSCARI ARMENIACUM
Grape Hyacinth

Often seen outdoors but rarely recommended in house plant books. It is still a good choice — plant in September for January-March flowers. The usual species is **M. armeniacum** (8 in., blue flowers with white rims) — for sky blue flowers pick **M. botryoides** (6 in.).

Muscari armeniacum

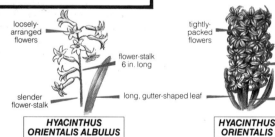

loosely-arranged flowers

flower-stalk 6 in. long

slender flower-stalk

long, gutter-shaped leaf

HYACINTHUS ORIENTALIS ALBULUS
Roman Hyacinth

tightly-packed flowers

flower-stalk 6–9 in. long

thick flower-stalk

HYACINTHUS ORIENTALIS
Dutch Hyacinth

Hyacinthus orientalis Amsterdam

The Dutch or Common Hyacinth is the most popular of all indoor bulbs. The leafless flower-stalks bear 30 or more crowded bell-like flowers with a fragrance that can fill a room. Each bulb bears a single stalk and the waxy 1–2 in. long blooms last for 2–3 weeks. Bulbs specially prepared for Christmas blooming should be planted in September — bulbs for January-March flowering are planted in October. There are scores of varieties — the range of colours is demonstrated by **L'Innocence** (white), **Yellow Hammer** (yellow), **Lady Derby** (pink), **Jan Bos** (red), **Ostara** (blue) and **Amethyst** (violet). Roman Hyacinths differ in a number of ways — 2 or 3 stalks are produced by each bulb and the flowers are smaller and less tightly packed. The flower-stalks are thinner and the colour range is restricted to white, pink and blue. Plant in August-September for December-January flowering. A third group, the Multiflora Hyacinths, bear several flower-stalks per bulb.

Galanthus Neil Frazer

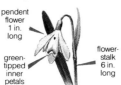
pendent
flower
1 in.
long

green-
tipped
inner
petals

flower-
stalk
6 in.
long

GALANTHUS NIVALIS
Snowdrop

Planting time is September — flowering time is January. The one you are most likely to see is the Common Snowdrop (**G. nivalis**). The best variety is **S. Arnott** (9 in.) — for double flowers choose **flore pleno.** The tallest Snowdrop is **G. elwesii** (10 in.).

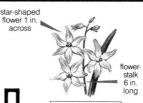
star-shaped
flower 1 in.
across

flower-
stalk
6 in.
long

CHIONODOXA LUCILIAE
Glory of the Snow

The popular Chionodoxa is **C. luciliae** — 10 white-centred, blue starry flowers appear on each slender stalk in late winter. **C. sardensis** has all-blue flowers, and the largest blooms (1½ in. across) are borne by **C. gigantea.** Plant the bulbs in September for February flowers.

Chionodoxa sardensis

Convallaria majalis

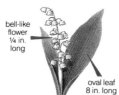
bell-like
flower
¼ in.
long

oval leaf
8 in. long

CONVALLARIA MAJALIS
Lily of the Valley

The dainty white bells and heavy fragrance are well known. For Christmas flowers you will have to buy specially prepared crowns ('pips') and plant a month before. Alternatively, lift crowns from outdoor plants and pot up in October for blooming in February.

star-shaped
flower 1 in.
across

flower-
stalk
3 in.
long

ERANTHIS HYEMALIS
Winter Aconite

Many of the bulbs in this section are instantly recognisable by the average gardener, but not this one. The bright yellow flowers have a frilly, leafy collar — plant in September for flowering in January alongside the Snowdrops. For 2 in. flowers grow **E. tubergenii.**

Eranthis tubergenii

Gladiolus primulinus Robin

trumpet-shaped
flower 3 in.
across

flower-stalk
2 ft long

GLADIOLUS COLUMBINE

Gladioli are not usually thought of as indoor bulbs, and the large-flowering types are not suitable. Choose one of the Primulinus or the Miniature Hybrids, such as **Columbine** or **Bo Peep,** or pick a low-growing species such as **G. colvillii** (1–2 ft).

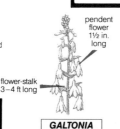
pendent
flower
1½ in.
long

flower-stalk
3–4 ft long

GALTONIA CANDICANS
Summer Hyacinth

This imposing plant is in marked contrast to the many dainty dwarfs in this section. Bulbs are planted in large pots in September and each flower-stalk bears 20 or more white bells in May-June. The strap-like leaves are 2 ft long.

Galtonia candicans

● IMPATIENS

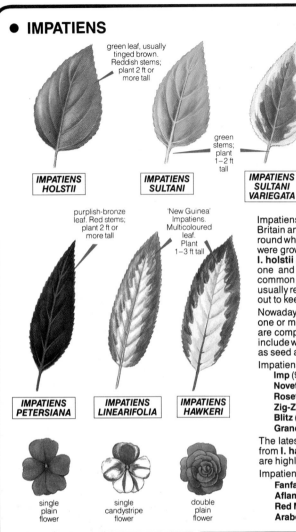

green leaf, usually tinged brown. Reddish stems; plant 2 ft or more tall

IMPATIENS HOLSTII

green stems; plant 1–2 ft tall

IMPATIENS SULTANI

IMPATIENS SULTANI VARIEGATA

flat-faced flower 1–2 in. across — long spur at rear

leaf 3 in. long

stems brittle and succulent, 1–3 ft long

IMPATIENS WALLERANA
Busy Lizzie
(Patient Lucy)

purplish-bronze leaf. Red stems; plant 2 ft or more tall

IMPATIENS PETERSIANA

single plain flower

'New Guinea' Impatiens. Multicoloured leaf. Plant 1–3 ft tall

IMPATIENS LINEARIFOLIA

single candystripe flower

IMPATIENS HAWKERI

double plain flower

Impatiens has long been grown on both sides of the Atlantic. Busy Lizzie in Britain and Patient Lucy in the U.S., this plant bears flowers almost all year round when cared for properly. Until fairly recently it was the species which were grown. There was (and still is) much confusion over their names — **I. holstii** and **I. sultani** have green leaves, **I. petersiana** is the red-leaved one and all are occasionally grouped together as **I. wallerana**. The common characteristics are a somewhat straggly growth habit and flowers, usually red, which are no more than 2 in. in diameter. Tips must be pinched out to keep the plant bushy and staking may be necessary.

Nowadays it is much more usual to grow the Impatiens Hybrids which have one or more of the species mentioned above as parents. These varieties are compact (½ – 1 ft) and the flower colour range has been extended to include white, orange, purple, pink, red and bicolours. Many can be bought as seed and raised at home.

Impatiens Hybrids:
Imp (9 in.) single, plain flowers — mixed colours.
Novette (6 in.) single, plain flowers — mixed colours.
Rosette (6 in.) semi-double and double, plain flowers — mixed colours.
Zig-Zag (9 in.) single, candystripe flowers — white plus orange or red.
Blitz (6 in.) single, plain flowers — mixed colours, very free-flowering.
Grand Prix (9 in.) single, plain flowers — mixed colours, very large blooms.

The latest introductions are the Impatiens New Guinea Hybrids evolved from **I. hawkeri** or **I. linearifolia**. The plants are 1–3 ft tall and the leaves are highly decorative. Flowers are often large.

Impatiens New Guinea Hybrids:
Fanfare leaves yellow/green — flowers pink.
Aflame leaves yellow/green/red — flowers pink.
Red Magic leaves bronzy — flowers red.
Arabesque leaves yellow/green/red — flowers pink.

Impatiens sultani variegata

Impatiens Zig-Zag

Impatiens Fanfare

● PRIMULAS

Tender species

yellow-eyed flower ½ in. across

flower-stalk 1½ ft long

oval, toothed leaf

PRIMULA MALACOIDES
Fairy Primrose

green-eyed flower 1–1½ in. across

flower-stalk 1 ft long

heart-shaped, coarse leaf

PRIMULA OBCONICA
Poison Primrose

frilly flower 1–1½ in. across

flower-stalk 1 ft long

lobed, toothed leaf

PRIMULA SINENSIS
Chinese Primrose

fragrant flower ¾ in. across

flower-stalk 1 ft long

powdery, toothed leaf

PRIMULA KEWENSIS

Primulas bear large numbers of flowers from December to March. Two garden types are grown indoors to brighten up the winter windowsill — the Common Primrose (**P. vulgaris** or **P. acaulis**) with its large flowers in white, yellow, red or blue clustered in a rosette of leaves, and the Polyanthus (**P. variabilis**) with its bright and often bicoloured flowers clustered on stout 1 ft stalks.

P. malacoides is the most popular of the tender types which are grown as temporary pot plants. The fragrant, small flowers in white, pink, purple or red are arranged in tiers on slender stalks. The flowers of **P. obconica** are large, fragrant and available in a wide range of colours, but the leaves can cause a rash on sensitive skins. The yellow-eyed **P. sinensis** is available in white, pink, red, orange and purple — the popular varieties have red, frilly-edged petals. **P. kewensis** is unmistakable — it is the only yellow-flowering tender Primula.

Garden species

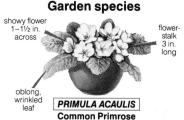

showy flower 1–1½ in. across

flower-stalk 3 in. long

oblong, wrinkled leaf

PRIMULA ACAULIS
Common Primrose

Primula malacoides

Primula obconica

Primula kewensis

● HEATHERS

Erica caniculata

tubular flower ¼ in. across

plant 2 ft tall

needle-like leaf ¾ in. long

ERICA HYEMALIS
French Heather

globular flower ⅛ in. across

plant 1½ ft tall

needle-like leaf ¼ in. long

ERICA GRACILIS
Cape Heath

The Cape Heath and its close relatives are bought in bloom, generally for Christmas, and are then discarded once the flowering period is over. There are needle-like leaves and masses of small flowers — **E. gracilis** with its pink or purple blooms is more popular than the larger-flowering **E. hyemalis**. The Christmas Heather (**E. canaliculata**) bears tiny white blooms with black centres. There is a midsummer-flowering heather — the white or mauve **E. ventricosa** (2 ft).

● MINIATURE ROSES

flowers single, semi-double or double

plant 6–12 in. high

flower ½–1½ in. across

ROSA CHINENSIS MINIMA
Miniature Rose
(Fairy Rose)

You will have no difficulty at all in recognising a Miniature Rose in bloom. It looks just like an ordinary garden variety scaled down to size — the same leaves, the same wide range of colours and flower-shapes, the same range of fragrance. With such properties and with our traditional love of the rose you would expect these hybrids of **R. chinensis minima (R. roulettii)** to be popular, but they are not. People have tried them as pot plants and have been disappointed. The secret is to choose a variety listed as 12 in. tall or less, pick a plant grown from a cutting or micro-cutting rather than a grafted rose, and treat as an indoor/outdoor plant — put it outdoors in autumn and bring indoors again in late winter.

Baby Darling (double, orange and pink, no fragrance, 12 in.)
Judy Fischer (double, pink, no fragrance, 9 in.)
Yellow Doll (double, pale yellow, fragrant, 10 in.)
Starina (double, vermilion, fragrant, 10 in.)
New Penny (double, coppery-pink, no fragrance, 9 in.)
Cinderella (double, silvery-pink, slight fragrance, 10 in.)

SINGLE
less than 8 petals

SEMI-DOUBLE
8–20 petals

DOUBLE
more than 20 petals

Rosa Baby Darling

Rosa Judy Fischer

Rosa Yellow Doll

● GLOXINIAS

upturned bell-shaped flower 3 in. across

oval, velvety leaf 9 in. long

SINNINGIA SPECIOSA
Gloxinia

The showy **S. speciosa** hybrids are known as Gloxinias. They can be raised from seed or tubers, but they are usually bought in bud as gift plants, lasting about 2 months indoors. The large trumpets are about 2 in. long, grouped on stalks arising from the heart of the leaf rosette. The velvety blooms are bold and colourful — white, pink, red or purple in various combinations. The petal edges are either plain or ruffled and multi-lobed (double) varieties are available.

Gregor Mendel (double, red with white edge)
Emperor Frederick (single, red with white edge)
Duchess of York (single, violet with white edge)
Mont Blanc (single, white)
Red Tiger (single, white with red spots)

Sinningia speciosa Gregor Mendel

● BROMELIADS

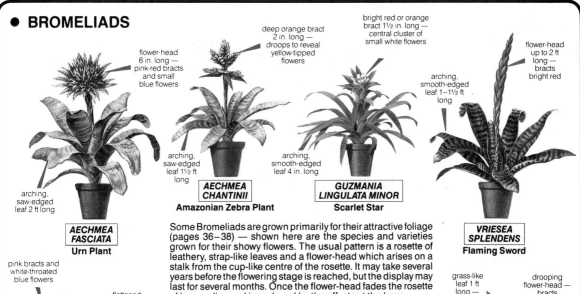

flower-head
6 in. long —
pink-red bracts
and small
blue flowers

deep orange bract
2 in. long —
droops to reveal
yellow-tipped
flowers

bright red or orange
bract 1½ in. long —
central cluster of
small white flowers

flower-head
up to 2 ft
long —
bracts
bright red

arching,
saw-edged
leaf 1½ ft
long

arching,
smooth-edged
leaf 4 in. long

arching,
smooth-edged
leaf 1–1½ ft
long

arching,
saw-edged
leaf 2 ft long

**AECHMEA
CHANTINII**
Amazonian Zebra Plant

**GUZMANIA
LINGULATA MINOR**
Scarlet Star

**AECHMEA
FASCIATA**
Urn Plant

**VRIESEA
SPLENDENS**
Flaming Sword

pink bracts and
white-throated
blue flowers

flattened
flower-head
9–12 in. long

grass-like
leaf 1 ft
long —
reddish in
good light

drooping
flower-head —
bracts
3 in. long

grass-
like
leaf
1 ft
long

Some Bromeliads are grown primarily for their attractive foliage (pages 36–38) — shown here are the species and varieties grown for their showy flowers. The usual pattern is a rosette of leathery, strap-like leaves and a flower-head which arises on a stalk from the cup-like centre of the rosette. It may take several years before the flowering stage is reached, but the display may last for several months. Once the flower-head fades the rosette of leaves dies and is replaced by the offsets at the base.

There are exceptions. **Billbergia nutans** has grassy leaves and young specimens flower quite readily. **B. windii** is similar but larger. The two most popular Tillandsias also have grassy leaves like the well-known Billbergias, but their flowers are quite different. **T. lindenii** is illustrated — **T. cyanea** has a green and more compact flower-head with flowers which are all-blue.

The Aechmeas are typical Bromeliads with leathery, arching leaves and a distinct central 'vase'. **A. fasciata** (**A. rhodocyanea**) is by far the most popular, but there are others. **A. chantinii** has colourful leaves as well as showy flowers and **A. caudata** has branching heads of yellow flowers. The Vrieseas are also typical Bromeliads with **V. splendens** (**V. speciosa**) as the best-known species. There are a number of others available, such as the giant **V. regina** and compact ones like **V. minor** and **V. psittacina**. Guzmania is becoming more widely known, especially the compact **G. lingulata minor**. There is a wide variety of flower-forms — strap-like red or orange bracts like **Amaranth, Grand Prix** and **minor**, 'flaming swords' such as **bertenonia** and yellow-tipped flowers like **Marlebeca**.

**TILLANDSIA
LINDENII**
Blue-flowered Torch

**BILLBERGIA
NUTANS**
Queen's Tears

Aechmea fasciata

Billbergia windii

Vriesea carinata

● FUCHSIAS

plant 1–3 ft high

slightly serrated leaf 1–2 in. long

flower 1½–3 in. long

FUCHSIA HYBRIDA

Fuchsia is deservedly a popular house plant. The pendent flowers are borne in profusion on bushy plants — each bell-like bloom in white, pink, red or purple with swept-back sepals giving a hooped-skirt effect. There are hundreds of named hybrids — in nearly all cases the colour is derived from both the showy sepals and petals, which may or may not be the same colour. This is the familiar Fuchsia Hybrid with single, semi-double or double bells on soft-stemmed bushes. To induce bushiness, pinch out the tip after 3 sets of leaves have formed. When each of the resulting side shoots has developed 3 sets of leaves, repeat the pinching-out operation. Remove dead flowers to promote bud formation.

In addition to the familiar hooped-skirt types, there are the Clustered Hybrids or Honeysuckle Fuchsias, generally derived from **F. triphylla.** Here the colour of the bloom comes from the sepals — the petals are either insignificant or absent.

Fuchsias are usually grown as bushes, although the trailing types are widely used in hanging baskets (see page 78). It is possible to train a vigorous upright variety as a standard by staking and removing all side shoots, but this will take several seasons and is more suited to the conservatory than to the living room.

SINGLE HYBRIDS	SEMI-DOUBLE HYBRIDS	DOUBLE HYBRIDS	CLUSTERED HYBRIDS

SINGLE HYBRIDS

Winston Churchill
(pink sepals, purple petals)
Citation
(pink sepals, white petals)
Bon Accord
(white sepals, lilac petals)
Checkerboard
(red and white sepals, red petals)
Brutus
(red sepals, purple petals)

SEMI-DOUBLE HYBRIDS

Snowcap
(red sepals, white petals)
Tennessee Waltz
(pink sepals, lilac petals)
Texas Longhorn
(red sepals, white petals)
Whirlaway
(white sepals, white petals)
Satellite
(red sepals, white petals)

DOUBLE HYBRIDS

Dollar Princess
(red sepals, lilac petals)
Fascination
(pink sepals, pink petals)
Midge
(rose sepals, pink petals)
Alice Hoffman
(red sepals, white petals)
Brigadoon
(red sepals, purple petals)

CLUSTERED HYBRIDS

Gartenmeister Bonstedt
(salmon-orange sepals)
Swanley Yellow
(orange sepals)
Leverkusen
(red sepals)
Thalia
(deep pink sepals)
Traudchen Bonstedt
(pale salmon sepals)

Fuchsia Winston Churchill

Fuchsia Texas Longhorn

Fuchsia Traudchen Bonstedt

● CINERARIAS

daisy-like flower 1–3 in. across

plant ¾–2½ ft tall

heart-shaped leaf up to 8 in. across

underside usually purple

SENECIO CRUENTUS
(SENECIO HYBRIDUS)
Cineraria

Cinerarias can be bought in bud between December and May to brighten up the home with their massed blooms for 4–6 weeks. After flowering is over they are thrown away. The blooms are borne in crowded heads about 9 in. across. You can find practically any colour apart from yellow — a prominent white eye is usually present. The soft leaves are rather woolly and the growth habit is compact or branching, depending on the variety chosen. Most of the commercial types belong to the **multiflora nana** strain — the **grandiflora** strain has impressive flowers but staking may be necessary. The **double** and **stellata** groups are much less common — the stellatas are branching plants.

Exhibition Mixed (grandiflora strain. Height 1½ ft)
Spring Glory (multiflora nana strain. Height 9 in.)
Gaytime (multiflora nana strain. Height 10 in.)
Triumph (multiflora nana strain. Height 1 ft)
Gubler's Mixed (double strain. Height 1½ ft)
Mixed Star (double strain. Height 2 ft)

GRANDIFLORA
bloom 2–3 in.
plant 1½–2 ft

DOUBLE
bloom 2 in.
plant 1–2 ft

MULTIFLORA NANA
bloom 1–2 in.
plant ¾–1¼ ft

STELLATA
bloom 1–1½ in.
plant 1½–2½ ft

Senecio cruentus Exhibition Mixed

Senecio cruentus Spring Glory

Senecio cruentus Gubler's Mixed

● EPIPHYLLUMS

notched stem 2 ft long

funnel-shaped flower 4–6 in. across

EPIPHYLLUM ACKERMANII
Orchid Cactus

The Epiphyllums are untidy plants, the strap-shaped stems sprawling outwards unless staked when in flower. This lack of an attractive growth habit is more than made up for by the flowers — flaring, multi-petalled trumpets which can be as large as a saucer. Nearly all the commercial varieties are hybrids of **E. ackermanii** — day-flowering plants which are available in a wide range of shades. The white, night-flowering Epiphyllums are hybrids of **E. cooperi** — the 5 in. flowers are very fragrant.

This cactus is closely related to the Easter and Christmas Cacti (see page 79) and like them will bloom every year with proper treatment. The range of colours is illustrated by **London Glory** (red), **Gloria** (orange), **Little Sister** (white), **Midnight** (purple), **Reward** (yellow), **Padre** (pink) . . . but no blue.

Epiphyllum Sabra

● GARDEN ANNUALS

There are generally two sources for the living floral display in our homes — plants are either bought in pots or bulbs are planted in bowls in autumn. Yet many of the flowering pot plants and a few of the foliage house plants described earlier in this book can be quite easily raised from seed. Examples are Cuphea, Solanum, Fuchsia, Gloxinia, Exacum, Browallia, Cyperus and Fatsia.

A number of popular pot plants, such as Celosia, Impatiens, Calceolaria, Schizanthus, Salpiglossis and Thunbergia are sometimes planted outdoors in the garden, but they are usually better known as pot plants for indoor use. On the other hand there are many popular garden annuals which can be grown as pot plants but are not generally used for this purpose — it is these 'Garden Annuals' which are described here.

You can, of course, raise these annuals from seed at home, using the windowsill if you do not have a greenhouse. Usually, however, you will want only a few plants and so it is often easier to buy them as seedlings in small pots in spring and then repot them at home. The expected time of flowering for such spring-sown plants is listed for each type — sowing some of these varieties in autumn instead of spring will produce earlier flowers.

AGERATUM HOUSTONIANUM
Ageratum

Height 8 in. In flower May-October. Pick a compact blue (**Blue Mink** or **Blue Blazer**). Or choose **Summer Snow** (white) and **Fairy Pink** (rose).

ANTIRRHINUM MAJUS
Snapdragon

Height 9 in. In flower June-October. Choose one of the dwarf varieties — **Magic Carpet, Floral Carpet** or **Tom Thumb.** Pinch out tip when 3 in. high.

CALENDULA OFFICINALIS
Pot Marigold

Height 1–2 ft. In flower May-October. Colours range from pale cream to deep orange. The best compact variety is the 1 ft **Fiesta Gitana.**

CENTAUREA CYANUS
Cornflower

Height 1 ft. In flower May-September. Choose a dwarf variety such as **Polka Dot** or **Jubilee Gem.** The grassy leaves are grey-green.

CLARKIA ELEGANS
Clarkia

Height 1½ ft. In flower June-October (March-April if sown in September). Available in white, pink, red and purple. **C. pulchella** (1 ft) is a daintier species.

CONVOLVULUS TRICOLOR
Dwarf Morning Glory

Height 9 in. In flower May-September. Bright-coloured trumpets on bushy plants — sow the compact **Blue Flash** or **Rainbow Flash.** Remove dead flowers.

GODETIA GRANDIFLORA
Godetia

Height 9 in.–1½ ft. In flower June-September (February-May if sown in September). Choose a short, bushy variety such as **Sybil Sherwood** or **Kelvedon Glory.**

IBERIS UMBELLATA
Candytuft

Height 9 in. In flower January-March if sown in summer. **Fairy Mixture** will give a variety of white, pink and red fragrant flowers.

IPOMOEA TRICOLOR
Morning Glory

Height 6 ft. In flower June-September. Each large trumpet-shaped flower lasts only a day — choose **Heavenly Blue** (white-eyed bloom) or **Flying Saucers** (blue and white stripes).

LATHYRUS ODORATUS
Sweet Pea

Height 1 ft. In flower June-October. Grow a dwarf variety — no support will be needed. **Bijou, Little Sweethearts** and **Patio** are examples.

LINUM GRANDIFLORUM
Flax

Height 1 ft. In flower June-August. The best one to choose is Scarlet Flax (**L. grandiflorum rubrum**). For white flowers grow **album.**

LOBELIA ERINUS
Lobelia

Height 4–8 in. In flower May-September. The deep blue variety is **Mrs Clibran Improved** — for hanging baskets grow **Sapphire** or **Cascade Mixed.**

MATTHIOLA INCANA
Stock

Height 1–2 ft. In flower December-May if sown in summer. For a long flowering season sow both **Brompton** and **Ten Week** strains. Excellent for fragrance.

MESEMBRYANTHEMUM CRINIFLORUM
Livingstone Daisy

Height 4–6 in. In flower June-September. Usually sold as a multicoloured mixture — **M. Lunette** is all yellow. A windowsill plant — direct sunlight is necessary.

MYOSOTIS ALPESTRIS
Forget-me-not

Height 6 in.–1 ft. In flower March-April if sown in summer and kept outdoors until frosts arrive. Compact varieties are best — **Ultramarine** (deep blue) or **Carmine King** (pink).

NEMESIA STRUMOSA
Nemesia

Height 9 in. In flower May-August (January-February if sown in July). Sow **Carnival** or **Sparklers** mixture. Grow numerous plants in a large container for a bold multicoloured display.

NICOTIANA HYBRIDA
Tobacco Plant

Height 9 in.–1½ ft. In flower May-September. Buy a day-flowering compact hybrid, such as **Tinkerbelle, Nicki Mixed, Red Devil** or **Domino Mixed.**

PETUNIA HYBRIDA
Petunia

Height 6 in. –1½ ft. In flower May-October. Catalogues offer a wide range of single and double varieties in a large and varied assortment of colours and patterns.

PHLOX DRUMMONDII
Annual Phlox

Height 6–9 in. In flower June-September. Pick from the **nana compacta** group — examples include **Twinkle, Beauty Mixed** and **Dwarf Petticoat.**

SALVIA SPLENDENS
Salvia

Height 9 in. –1 ft. In flower June-September. Choose a compact variety such as **Blaze of Fire** or **Scarlet Pygmy** (red). **Dress Parade Mixed** provides various colours.

TAGETES ERECTA
African Marigold

Height 1–2 ft. In flower May-September. Grow one of the dwarf varieties which rarely exceed 1½ ft — **Gay Ladies, Inca Yellow, Space Age Mixed,** etc.

TAGETES PATULA
French Marigold

Height 6–9 in. In flower May-September. All sorts of blends of yellow, orange, red and mahogany in single and double blooms are listed in catalogues.

TROPAEOLUM MAJUS
Nasturtium

Height 6 in. –1 ft. In flower May-September. The **Gleam** hybrids are the most popular choice, especially for hanging baskets. Dwarfs (6 in.) are also available.

VERBENA HYBRIDA
Verbena

Height 6 in. –1 ft. In flower June-September. Pick one of the compact varieties — **Sparkle, Springtime** and **Dwarf Compact Mixed** are all good choices.

VIOLA TRICOLOR
Pansy

Height 6–9 in. In flower February-November, depending on variety and date of sowing. For the largest flowers, choose one of the **Swiss Giants. Floral Dance** is winter flowering.

VIOLA HYBRIDA
Viola

Height 6–9 in. In flower February-November, depending on date of sowing. Plants remain in bloom for 2–3 months. Various colours, such as **Blue Heaven** and **Yellow Bedder.**

ZINNIA ELEGANS
Zinnia

Height 6 in. –1½ ft. Select a low-growing strain, not one of the 2½ ft giants. Good ones include **Thumbelina, Pulchino, Peter Pan** and **Lilliput.**

Calendula officinalis

Lobelia erinus

Petunia hybrida

Phlox drummondii

Tagetes erecta

Tropaeolum majus

• ORCHIDS

The old idea that Orchids are only for skilled growers with a greenhouse or conservatory is not true. Several types will grow quite happily under ordinary room conditions — provided you remember that each type has its own special needs.

In general, Orchids need bright light and high humidity. To ensure moist air the plants should be kept in a glass case (terrarium) or the pot should be placed in a tray of wet pebbles. All need a special orchid compost and some will need a period of rest (almost dry compost) for part of the year — some also need constant warmth. So choose with care and seek advice from either a book, catalogue or an expert. If you follow the rules the 'easy' ones (**Cymbidium, Coelogyne, Odontoglossum, Paphiopedilum, Vuylstekeara,** etc.) can be grown in the living room. Flowers of the most popular house plant Orchids are shown here — others include **Dendrobium, Oncidium, Lycaste** and **Vanda.**

CATTLEYA
Corsage Orchid

Waxy, beautiful flowers 4–6 in. across. A terrarium plant as it needs high humidity and a fairly constant temperature.

CYMBIDIUM

The miniature Cymbidium hybrids are the most popular house plant Orchids. Waxy flower 1½ in. across — succeeds under ordinary room conditions.

flower has 3 sepals and 3 petals. Lowest petal is the lip — this is always different from the others

COELOGYNE

Fragrant flower 2–4 in. across. **C. cristata** (illustrated above) is the easy one. Winter rest needed.

MILTONIA
Pansy Orchid

Velvety, pansy-like flower 2–4 in. across. Not easy under room conditions — dislikes temperature changes.

ODONTOGLOSSUM
Tiger Orchid

O. grande (flower 6 in. across) is the popular one shown here — not difficult if good light, high humidity and winter rest are provided.

most Orchids have a thickened stem-base — the pseudobulb. Shapes vary — oval, cylindrical or globular

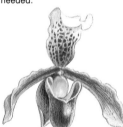

PAPHIOPEDILUM
Slipper Orchid

Many hybrids available — sometimes listed as **Cypripedium.** Prominently-pouched flower 2-4 in. across — suitable for room cultivation.

PHALAENOPSIS
Moth Orchid

Flat-faced flower 2 in. across — numerous blooms borne on arching stalks. Quite fussy — needs steady temperature and high humidity.

VUYLSTEKEARA

Popular man-made hybrid. Flower about 4 in. across — has the same requirements as Odontoglossum, one of its parents.

Cymbidium Rievaulx Hamsey

Paphiopedilum Hybriden

Phalaenopsis Happy Rose

● BEGONIAS

Tuber-grown types

single or double flower 2 in. across

pointed, serrated leaf 4 in. long

BEGONIA MULTIFLORA

pointed, serrated leaf 6–9 in. long

single or double flower 3–5 in. across

BEGONIA TUBERHYBRIDA

Bushy types

white or pink flower 1 in. across

glossy, round leaf 3 in. across

green stems

BEGONIA CHEIMANTHA
Lorraine Begonia

flower 2 in. across

glossy, round leaf 3 in. across

red stems

BEGONIA HIEMALIS

single or double flower 1 in. across

round, waxy leaf 2 in. across

BEGONIA SEMPERFLORENS
Wax Begonia

serrated, glossy leaf 1½ in. long

plant 3 ft high

pink or red flower 1 in. across

BEGONIA FUCHSIOIDES
Fuchsia Begonia

pale pink flower ½ in. across

hairy leaf 8 in. long

plant 2 ft high

underside red

BEGONIA HAAGEANA
Elephant Ear Begonia

deep pink flower ½ in. across

lobed, serrated leaf 3 in. long

green blotched with red

BEGONIA SERRATIPETALA
Pink Spot Begonia

Cane-stemmed types

waxy flower ½ in. across

underside red

BEGONIA COCCINEA
Angel Wing Begonia

glossy, red-margined leaf 5 in. long

white-spotted leaf 5 in. long

pink flower ½ in. across

BEGONIA LUCERNA

glossy leaf 5 in. long

olive green blotched with white

BEGONIA ARGENTEO-GUTTATA
Trout Begonia

There is a bewildering range of Begonias which can be grown indoors. Some are cultivated mainly or solely for the beauty of their leaves or their pendulous growth habit — these are described elsewhere. Shown here are the upright Flowering Begonias.

The tuber-grown types are raised from tubers planted at home or are bought as house plants in bud. **B. tuberhybrida** is the favourite — 1 ft tall fleshy-stemmed plants which bear large and showy male flowers and smaller female ones. **B. multiflora** flowers are similar, but they are much more numerous and smaller.

Other Begonias are raised from seed or bought in pots. The **B. cheimantha** hybrids are old favourites for winter flowering — **Gloire de Lorraine** has been grown for many years. In recent years, however, the **Rieger-Elatior** hybrids of **B. hiemalis** have taken over as the most popular bushy Begonias. Named varieties include the red ones **Fireglow, Schwabenland** and **Heidi** — **Elfe** has pink flowers. The waxy-leaved **B. semperflorens** is another popular Begonia, its white, pink or red flowers appearing at any time of the year. The remaining bushy Begonias are much less common.

The cane-stemmed types produce tall bamboo-like stems which bear pendulous flower-heads. The 6 ft **B. lucerna** is the most popular.

Begonia Heidi

Begonia tuberhybrida Judy Langdon

● GERANIUMS

Pelargoniums (commonly called Geraniums) are amongst the most popular of all flowering house plants. There are two major groups, and by far the more widely grown is the Common, Zonal or Bedding Geranium. The bushy plants are usually 1–2 ft high, but some varieties can reach 4 ft or more. With care the flowering season can last nearly all year round — all they need is sun and rather dry compost.

The second group (the Regal or Martha Washington Geraniums) have more spectacular blooms — each flower is larger, frillier and more colourful than the Zonal Geranium. But there are drawbacks — they are less easy to grow, the flowering season is shorter and fewer blooms are borne.

Zonal Geraniums

brittle, thick stems

rounded leaf 3–4 in. across. Most varieties have a horseshoe marking or 'zone'

flower ½–1½ in. across. Single, semi-double and double are the usual forms. Colours — white, pink, orange, red and purple

 SINGLE

 STELLAR

 CACTUS

PELARGONIUM HORTORUM
(PELARGONIUM ZONALE)

Marechal MacMahon   Distinction

Mrs Pollock   Mrs Henry Cox

Standard varieties: Height 1–2 ft.
Propagate from cuttings taken in late summer.
P. **Paul Crampel** Bright red, single
P. **King of Denmark** Rose, semi-double
P. **Gustave Emich** Bright red, double
P. **Jane Campbell** Orange, single
P. **Queen of the Whites** White, single
P. **Vera Dillon** Purple, single
P. **Hermione** White, double
P. **Festiva Maxima** Purple, double
P. **Distinction** Red, single
P. **Mrs Pollock** Vermilion, single
P. **Mrs Henry Cox** Rose, single
P. **Gazelle** Pink, stellar

Irenes: Vigorous and free flowering.
Flowers semi-double — flower-heads larger than Standard varieties.
P. **Springtime** Salmon-pink
P. **Modesty** White
P. **Surprise** Pink
P. **Electra** Red with blue overtones
P. **Fire Brand** Red

Deacons: Compact. Flower-heads small but very numerous.
P. **Deacon Fireball** Bright red, double
P. **Mandarin** Orange, double
P. **Deacon Bonanza** Bright pink, double
P. **Deacon Coral Reef** Pink, double

Rosebuds: Small flowers, centre petals remaining unopened like miniature rosebuds.
P. **Red Rambler** Red
P. **Appleblossom Rosebud** Pink
P. **Rosebud Supreme** Red

Cactus: Petals narrow and twisted.
P. **Fire Dragon** Red
P. **Noel** White
P. **Tangerine** Orange

F_1 **Hybrids** raised from seed:
Can be bought as seeds or bedding plants.
P. **Cherie** Salmon-pink
P. **Ringo** Red
P. **Mustang** Red
P. **Bright Eyes** White-eyed red
P. **Sprinter** Red
P. **Carefree Mixed** Various colours

Miniatures and dwarfs: Height 9 in. or less.
P. **Red Black Vesuvius** Red
P. **Fantasia** White
P. **Pixie** Salmon
P. **Caligula** Red
P. **Grace Wells** Lilac
P. **Video** Various colours

Regal Geraniums

scalloped leaf with serrated edge 3 in. across

brittle, thin stems

flower 1½–2½ in. across. Petals are usually frilled, with splashes or lines of a second colour. Prominent eye often present. Colours — white, pink, orange, red and purple

PELARGONIUM DOMESTICUM
(PELARGONIUM GRANDIFLORUM)

Height 1–2 ft. Propagate from cuttings taken in late summer.
P. **Easter Greetings** Rose with brown blotches
P. **Aztec** White with pink blotches
P. **Lavender Grand Slam** Lavender with purple blotches
P. **Grandma Fischer** Orange with brown blotches
P. **Snowbank** White, frilled
P. **Geronimo** Red, frilled

P. **Applause** Pink, frilled
P. **Gay Nineties** White with purple blotches
P. **Elsie Hickman** Vermilion, pink and white
P. **Georgia Peach** Peach, frilled
P. **Carisbrooke** Rose-pink
P. **Sue Jarrett** Salmon-pink with maroon blotches
P. **Swabian Maid** Carmine-rose

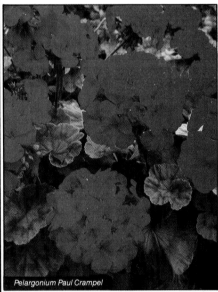
Pelargonium Paul Crampel

Pelargonium Carisbrooke

● LILIES

Lilies are generally regarded as garden flowers with no place in the home. It is true that their cultivation under room conditions is not as easy as outdoors or in the cold greenhouse, but there are several types which can be relied upon to succeed indoors.

The first task is to pick a bulb recommended for growing in the home — avoid the giants such as Lilium henryi and do not use basal-rooting species such as L. canadense and L. candidum. Some of the Species Lilies are suitable, but the best plan for the beginner is to choose one of the Hybrid Lilies.

You will need plenty of space and a 6 in. pot. Plant the bulb as soon as it is obtained in autumn. Specially-prepared Lilies will bloom in spring — untreated bulbs will flower in summer. Keep the pot outdoors or in a cool place until growth starts — do not move into a warm room until buds have formed. Some of the types listed below are described as half hardy — these should not be kept outdoors before bringing into the house.

You can buy pot-grown Lilies — the varieties are usually different from the types sold as bulbs in the catalogues or garden centres. Pot-grown Lilies include Easter Lily, Oriental Hybrids (Dominique, Darling, etc) and Asiatic Hybrids (Aristo, Symphony, etc). Some of the popular types sold as bulbs are listed below, but a good catalogue will contain many more.

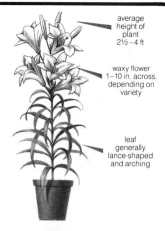

average height of plant 2½ – 4 ft

waxy flower 1 – 10 in. across, depending on variety

leaf generally lance-shaped and arching

BOWL SHAPED
The petals flare open to produce a wide bowl. The flowers are usually large.

L. auratum (Golden-rayed Lily) Height 4 – 5 ft. Flowers 8 – 10 in. across. White with yellow stripes and brown spots. Fragrant. Flowering period late summer.
L. speciosum (Japanese Lily) Height 3 – 4 ft. Flowers 3 – 5 in. across. White with red markings. Fragrant. Flowering period summer. Half hardy — grow indoors.
  Grand Commander — the best variety, petals deep red with paler edges.
L. Empress of China Height 3 – 4 ft. Flowers 8 in. across. White with dark red spots. Fragrant. Flowering period summer. Half hardy — grow indoors.

TRUMPET SHAPED
The petals are grouped together for part of the length of the flower to produce a basal tube.

L. longiflorum (Easter Lily) Height 3 ft. Flowers 5 in. across. White. Fragrant. Flowering period summer. Half hardy — grow indoors.
  Mount Everest — giant (6 ft) variety with large flowers.
L. regale (Regal Lily) Height 4 ft. Flowers 5 in. across. White with yellow throat. Fragrant. Flowering period summer.
  Royal Gold — all-yellow.
L. Mid-Century Hybrids Height 2 – 4 ft. Flowers 4 – 5 in. across. Yellow, orange or red — all spotted. Flowering period early summer.

Enchantment — orange-red, very popular	**Brandywine** — apricot
Destiny — lemon-yellow	**Prosperity** — pale yellow
Cinnabar — maroon-red	**Connecticut King** — gold
Paprika — crimson	**Chinook** — orange
Sterling Silver — cream	**Tabasco** — dark red

L. Golden Splendor Height 4 ft. Flowers 6 in. across. Gold; maroon-striped on reverse. Flowering period summer.

TURK'S-CAP SHAPED
The petals are rolled and swept back. The flowers are usually small.

L. pumilum Height 1 – 2 ft. Flowers 2 in. across. Red. Flowering period early summer.
L. Fiesta Hybrids Height 3 – 4 ft. Flowers 3 in. across. Various colours. Flowering period summer.
L. Citronella Height 3 ft. Flowers 3 in. across. Yellow with black dots. Flowering period summer.

Lilium longiflorum

Lilium Destiny

● AFRICAN VIOLETS

violet-like flower usually 1–1½ in. across. White, blue, pink, red and purple — bicolours available

fleshy foliage with velvety surface

round or heart-shaped leaf usually 2–4 in. across

SAINTPAULIA IONANTHA
African Violet

For many the African Violet is the queen of house plants. It is compact enough for even the smallest room, and yet *en masse* will provide a sheet of eye-catching colour. Its great attraction is that it will bloom and bloom again if you follow the rules — even a beginner can expect several flushes a year and an expert with artificial lighting can keep some varieties in bloom almost all year round.

There are thousands of varieties with a bewildering assortment of flower forms and colours. It is therefore surprising that this great favourite is a relative newcomer. The first plant was found in Africa in 1890 and its offspring were shown in Europe in 1893. The first commercial plants were raised in Germany and it was the seeds from Germany and England which started the U.S. interest in the 1920s. The first commercial hybrid offered was **Blue Boy** and from this simple beginning a vast host of other hybrids have sprung. Once the African Violet was a notoriously difficult plant — modern varieties are much easier to grow. The search goes on for the yellow and the orange, the highly scented and the boldly striped.

The **Rhapsodie** strain contains varieties which have dominated the British and Continental scene for years. Reasonably easy to grow and propagate, the upright plants produce an abundance of flowers.

Diana African Violets (**Diana Blue, Diana Double Pink**, etc) belong to the **Harmonie** strain. This strain is noted for large, long-lasting blooms and vigorous growth.

Rococo varieties (**Rococo Pink** and **Rococo Blue**) are compact plants with girl-type foliage and double flowers.

The **Ballet** strain contains varieties which are extremely popular in the U.S. These standard-sized hybrids are reasonably easy to grow and propagate.

The **Du Pont** strain (**Du Pont Silver Blue, Du Pont Blue**, etc) are giants, with leaves and flowers which are much larger than normal. Other giant-flowered varieties exist, such as **Wonderland, Confederate Beauty**, together with the **Amazon** and **Supreme** strains.

The **Fringette** strain is noted for its frilled flowers. **Pink Fringette** bears long-lasting flowers well above the foliage. Frilled varieties are becoming increasingly popular — good examples are **Fancy Pants** (red and white), **Colorado** (magenta), **Miss Pretty** (pink and white) and **Maria** (pink).

White varieties lack popular appeal as African Violets are expected to be colourful. **Icefloe** has long been a popular double, **Snow White** and **White Lady** were the first of the American whites and **Chiffon Cream** is a modern English double.

Many bicolours are now available, both plain-edged and frilled. One of the first hybrids was **Bicolor**, with upper and lower petals in different colours. Today's bicolours have different colours on the same petal — examples are **Spring Sky, Painted Girl, Sunset**, and **China Cup**.

Plants with variegated foliage are rare — the best-known type is the American **Blue Boy-in-the-Snow**.

A number of varieties can be bought as seed and raised at home. These include **Blue Concerto, Grandiflora Pink, Blue Fairy Tale** and **Pink Shades**.

Micro-miniatures make an excellent novelty display, especially when grown in a wine-glass! **Pip Squeek** (bell-shaped flowers) is perhaps the best known — others include **Twinkle** (pink star-shaped flowers) and **Blue Imp** (blue star-shaped flowers).

The **Endurance** strain contains varieties named after Arctic explorers. As you would expect from the name these plants can withstand lower temperatures than other African Violets.

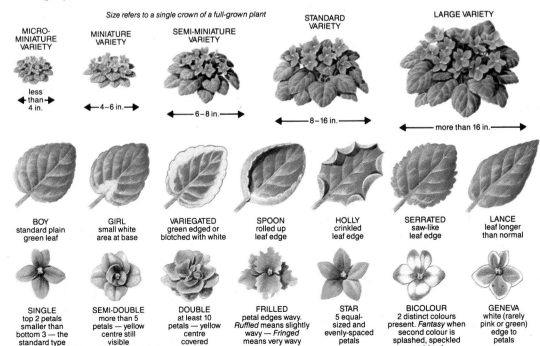

Size refers to a single crown of a full-grown plant

MICRO-MINIATURE VARIETY
less than 4 in.

MINIATURE VARIETY
4–6 in.

SEMI-MINIATURE VARIETY
6–8 in.

STANDARD VARIETY
8–16 in.

LARGE VARIETY
more than 16 in.

BOY
standard plain green leaf

GIRL
small white area at base

VARIEGATED
green edged or blotched with white

SPOON
rolled up leaf edge

HOLLY
crinkled leaf edge

SERRATED
saw-like leaf edge

LANCE
leaf longer than normal

SINGLE
top 2 petals smaller than bottom 3 — the standard type

SEMI-DOUBLE
more than 5 petals — yellow centre still visible

DOUBLE
at least 10 petals — yellow centre covered

FRILLED
petal edges wavy. *Ruffled* means slightly wavy — *Fringed* means very wavy

STAR
5 equal-sized and evenly-spaced petals

BICOLOUR
2 distinct colours present. *Fantasy* when second colour is splashed, speckled or striped

GENEVA
white (rarely pink or green) edge to petals

Saintpaulia ionantha Crimson Frost

Saintpaulia ionantha China Cup

Saintpaulia ionantha Top Job

Saintpaulia ionantha Diana Blue

Saintpaulia ionantha Rhapsodie Pink

Saintpaulia ionantha Rhapsodie

Saintpaulia ionantha Rococo Pink

Saintpaulia ionantha Fancy Pants

Saintpaulia ionantha Pip Squeek

● CHRYSANTHEMUMS

single or double flower 2–4 in. across

plant 1 ft high

dark green lobed leaf 3–5 in. long

CHRYSANTHEMUM MORIFOLIUM
Pot Chrysanthemum

single flower 2–3 in. across

plant 1–1½ ft high

grey-green ferny leaf 2–4 in. long

CHRYSANTHEMUM FRUTESCENS
Marguerite

plant 1–2 ft high

single flower 1 in. across

CHRYSANTHEMUM MORIFOLIUM CHARM
Charm Chrysanthemum

Decorative varieties of Chrysanthemum have been popular as greenhouse plants for many, many years and these are described in The Flower Expert. More recently the Pot Chrysanthemum has become a great favourite as a house plant. The dual techniques of controlling light and applying dwarfing compounds have enabled nurserymen to provide large-flowered plants all year round. Buy them with a few open blooms and a mass of buds which are showing colour. The plant should remain attractive for 6–8 weeks. Discard at this stage or plant out in the garden.

Marguerites are generally summer flowering — white, yellow and pink varieties are available. Charm Chrysanthemums have similar but smaller flowers, a drawback they more than make up for by the number of blooms produced and the ease with which they can be raised from seed. White, orange, yellow, pink and red strains are available. Least known of the house plant Chrysanthemums is the **Mini-Mum** (single flowers, 6–8 in. high).

Chrysanthemum morifolium Princess Anne

Chrysanthemum morifolium Charm Pink

● AZALEAS

open, bell-shaped flower 1½–2 in. across

plant 1–1½ ft high

leathery leaf 1½ in. long

underside hairy

funnel-shaped flower 1 in. across

glossy leaf 1–1½ in. long

RHODODENDRON SIMSII
(AZALEA INDICA)
Azalea
(Indian Azalea)

RHODODENDRON OBTUSUM
Japanese Azalea
(Kurume Azalea)

R. simsii is an extremely popular Christmas plant, bought as the flowers are beginning to open. With care it will bloom for many weeks and with skill it can be retained to provide a repeat display in the following year. The variety range covers single and double blooms in white, red, pink and orange. The Japanese Azalea **R. obtusum** is much less popular. The blooms are smaller and less numerous, but it has the distinct advantage of thriving quite happily as a garden shrub if planted out when flowering is over.

Rhododendron obtusum Coral Bells

● CYCLAMEN

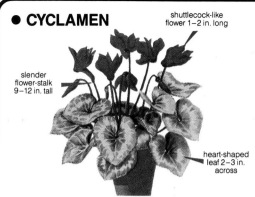

shuttlecock-like flower 1–2 in. long

slender flower-stalk 9–12 in. tall

heart-shaped leaf 2–3 in. across

CYCLAMEN PERSICUM
Cyclamen

Illustrated on the left is a typical example of the standard Cyclamen hybrid. The wild **C. persicum** of the Middle East has narrow, pink petals — the hybrids which first began to appear about 100 years ago are sometimes listed as **C. persicum giganteum**. These plants have wide petals which may be frilled and are available in many colours — white, pink, red, purple and salmon. Fragrant varieties are available and the foliage is usually edged, marbled or lined in white. This leaf patterning is sometimes bold enough to rival the flowers in display value.

Cyclamens are bought in vast numbers between autumn and early spring, with Christmas as the peak period. The plants should be in bud with perhaps a few open flowers — keep cool and moist, and the display will last for 2–3 months. You can save the tubers for planting in summer but it is usually better to buy fresh ones. You can also raise Cyclamen from seed, but germination is slow and erratic and you will have to wait about 15 months for blooms from an autumn sowing.

Once there were only standard-sized hybrids but now there are also dwarfs with pretty scented flowers on stalks which are only a few inches high.

Standard varieties: Height 9–12 in.
   Triumph strain. Large and abundant flowers. Attractive leaves.
   Rex strain. Compact plants. Leaves boldly marbled in silver — the best choice for foliage display.
   Ruffled strain. Fringed petals in pink, red and mauve.
   Decora strain. Noted for pastel shades (salmon, lavender, etc) and attractive foliage.
   Grandia strain. Large flowers with frilled and wavy petals.
   Firmament strain. Noted for early flowering.
   Fuzzy-Wuzzy strain. Bearded petals.
   Other standard varieties include **Cardinal** (red), **Cattleya** (lavender), **Pannevis** strain and the bicoloured **Victoria**.

Dwarf varieties: Height 7 in. or less
   Puppet strain. Scented flowers.
   Kaori strain. Scented flowers with distinct eye. Attractive foliage.
   Symphony strain. Scented flowers. Reputed to withstand central heating.
   Other dwarf varieties include **Mini-Sirius**, **Mini-Dresden** strain and **Mirabel** strain.

Cyclamen persicum Decora

Cyclamen persicum Suttons Puppet

● KALANCHOE

tubular flower ¼ in. across

plant 1 ft high

fleshy leaf 2 in. long

flower-head of 20–50 blooms

KALANCHOE BLOSSFELDIANA
Flaming Katy

By far the most popular Kalanchoe is **K. blossfeldiana** — a bushy, succulent-leaved plant which can be bought in flower at any time of the year. It is most frequently bought as a Christmas gift plant and the basic colour is red, but these days you can buy large hybrids in white, yellow, orange and lilac as well as red, bearing large heads on 18 in. high plants. At the other end of the scale the miniatures are growing in popularity — these compact plants grow about 6 in. high and bear glowing red flowers. Varieties include **Tom Thumb** and **Compact Lilliput** — **Vulcan** can be bought as seed as well as a pot-grown plant. The foliage of miniature and standard varieties turns reddish in bright light, and the floral display should last for 2–3 months. The plants are usually thrown away, but with care can be kept to produce a repeat display.

Kalanchoe blossfeldiana Vesuvius

● OTHER FLOWERING PLANTS

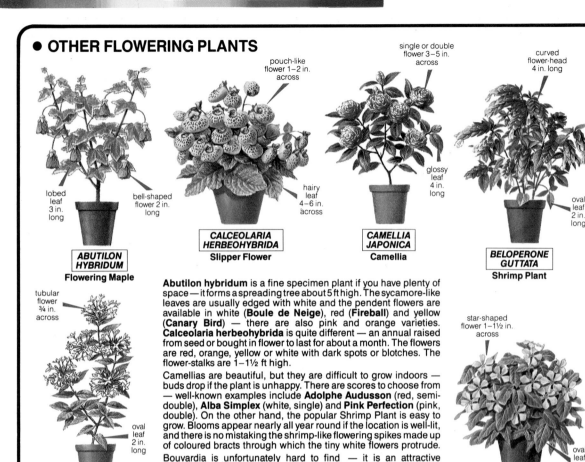

pouch-like flower 1–2 in. across

single or double flower 3–5 in. across

curved flower-head 4 in. long

lobed leaf 3 in. long

bell-shaped flower 2 in. long

hairy leaf 4–6 in. across

glossy leaf 4 in. long

oval leaf 2 in. long

ABUTILON HYBRIDUM
Flowering Maple

CALCEOLARIA HERBEOHYBRIDA
Slipper Flower

CAMELLIA JAPONICA
Camellia

BELOPERONE GUTTATA
Shrimp Plant

tubular flower ¾ in. across

oval leaf 2 in. long

BOUVARDIA DOMESTICA
Bouvardia

star-shaped flower 1–1½ in. across

oval leaf 2 in. long

CATHARANTHUS ROSEUS
(VINCA ROSEA)
Madagascar Periwinkle

Abutilon hybridum is a fine specimen plant if you have plenty of space — it forms a spreading tree about 5 ft high. The sycamore-like leaves are usually edged with white and the pendent flowers are available in white (**Boule de Neige**), red (**Fireball**) and yellow (**Canary Bird**) — there are also pink and orange varieties. **Calceolaria herbeohybrida** is quite different — an annual raised from seed or bought in flower to last for about a month. The flowers are red, orange, yellow or white with dark spots or blotches. The flower-stalks are 1–1½ ft high.

Camellias are beautiful, but they are difficult to grow indoors — buds drop if the plant is unhappy. There are scores to choose from — well-known examples include **Adolphe Audusson** (red, semi-double), **Alba Simplex** (white, single) and **Pink Perfection** (pink, double). On the other hand, the popular Shrimp Plant is easy to grow. Blooms appear nearly all year round if the location is well-lit, and there is no mistaking the shrimp-like flowering spikes made up of coloured bracts through which the tiny white flowers protrude. Bouvardia is unfortunately hard to find — it is an attractive evergreen which grows about 2 ft high. The fragrant flowers are borne in large clusters from midsummer to early winter. Varieties include **Mary** (white and pink) and **President Cleveland** (red). Catharanthus is also uncommon — a small bushy plant which bears masses of pink or lavender flowers in spring. White varieties are available.

Abutilon hybridum Michael

Beloperone guttata

Camellia japonica Florentine

single or double flower 2in. across

fragrant flower 1½ in. across

conical flower-head 6–9 in. long

red, pink or white flower-head 1 ft across

oval leaflet 2 in. long

grass-like leaf 2 in. long

lance-shaped leaf 4 in. long

lobed leaf 5 in. long

DAHLIA VARIABILIS
Pot Dahlia

DIANTHUS CHINENSIS
Annual Pink

CELOSIA PLUMOSA
Plume Flower

EUPHORBIA PULCHERRIMA
Poinsettia

tubular flower 1 in. across

bell-shaped flower 3 in. across

lance-shaped leaf 8 in. long

CESTRUM NOCTURNUM
Night Jessamine

Pot Dahlias are much, much less popular than Pot Chrysanthemums. They are beginning to appear at garden centres, and seed can be readily obtained. These plants are natural miniatures, not artificially dwarfed like their chrysanthemum counterparts. They grow about 1 ft high — varieties include **Figaro, Rigoletto, Redskin** and **Dahl-Face.** Dianthus is another plant better known in the garden than indoors, but Annual Pinks (**Dianthus chinensis**) and Carnations (**Dianthus caryophyllus**) are sometimes sold as pot plants and are easily raised from seed.

Celosia plumosa is a showy pot plant, growing about 2 ft high and bearing red or yellow plumes in summer. Dwarfs (8–12 in.) such as **Golden Plume** and **Kewpie** are available. **Celosia cristata** produces a velvety 'cockscomb' in yellow, orange or red in place of the plume of its better-known relative. **Euphorbia pulcherrima** is the well-known Poinsettia. The modern hybrid is a great improvement on the Poinsettias of 20 years ago. They are short (1–2 ft), long-lasting (2–6 months) and long-suffering under most conditions.

The Night Jessamines (**Cestrum nocturnum** and the smaller **C. parqui**) are grown for their night fragrance — the Day Jessamine (**C. diurnum**) is sweet-smelling during the day. Not all bear white flowers — **C. elegans** has pendent clusters of red blooms. The Kaffir Lily is an old favourite, the large leaves spreading out from the leek-like base and a cluster of 10–20 lily-like flowers opening in early spring. Orange is the usual colour, but there are red and yellow varieties.

strap-like leaf 1½ ft long

CLIVIA MINIATA
Kaffir Lily

Dahlia Figaro

Celosia cristata

Clivia miniata

● OTHER FLOWERING PLANTS continued

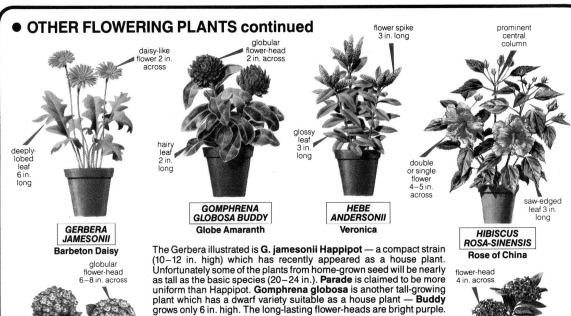

daisy-like flower 2 in. across

globular flower-head 2 in. across

flower spike 3 in. long

prominent central column

deeply-lobed leaf 6 in. long

hairy leaf 2 in. long

glossy leaf 3 in. long

double or single flower 4–5 in. across

saw-edged leaf 3 in. long

GERBERA JAMESONII
Barbeton Daisy

GOMPHRENA GLOBOSA BUDDY
Globe Amaranth

HEBE ANDERSONII
Veronica

HIBISCUS ROSA-SINENSIS
Rose of China

globular flower-head 6–8 in. across

oval, saw-edged leaf 4–6 in. long

HYDRANGEA MACROPHYLLA
Hydrangea
(Hortensia)

flower-head 4 in. across

tubular flower ½ in. across

glossy, leathery leaf 3–4 in. long

IXORA COCCINEA
Flame of the Woods

The Gerbera illustrated is **G. jamesonii Happipot** — a compact strain (10–12 in. high) which has recently appeared as a house plant. Unfortunately some of the plants from home-grown seed will be nearly as tall as the basic species (20–24 in.). **Parade** is claimed to be more uniform than Happipot. **Gomphrena globosa** is another tall-growing plant which has a dwarf variety suitable as a house plant — **Buddy** grows only 6 in. high. The long-lasting flower-heads are bright purple.

Several Hebes can be grown indoors, but the only ones you are likely to find are hybrids of **H. andersonii**. These evergreen shrubs grow about 3 ft high — varieties are available with white, violet or blue flowers. The most popular type is **variegata** (violet flowers, white-edged leaves). **Hibiscus rosa-sinensis** is another shrubby plant, but unlike Hebe it bears stunning individual blooms. Each one lasts only for a day or two, but with care the flowering season extends from spring to late summer and the bush will grow 5 ft high.

The ball-like flower-heads of **Hydrangea macrophylla** form a showy display in spring or summer. They last for about 6 weeks, after which the pot should be moved outdoors. White, pink, red and blue varieties are available — the blue ones need an acid compost. Staking will be necessary when the bush is in full flower. **Ixora coccinea** is an attractive but difficult shrub — not one for the novice. With care the large flower-heads in white, yellow, salmon, pink or red will last throughout the summer months. If you can keep the plant alive it will eventually reach a height of 3–4 ft.

Gerbera jamesonii Happipot

Hibiscus rosa-sinensis Holiday

Ixora coccinea

fragrant flower 2 in. across

willow-like leaf 6–8 in. long

NERIUM OLEANDER
Oleander

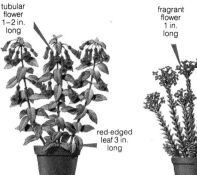

tubular flower 1–2 in. long

red-edged leaf 3 in. long

KOHLERIA ERIANTHA

fragrant flower 1 in. long

leathery leaf 1 in. long

ROCHEA COCCINEA
Crassula

rose-like flower 1–1½ in. across

cylindrical leaf ½ in. long

PORTULACA GRANDIFLORA
Sun Plant

flower-head 1–2 in. across

rough leaf 2 in. long

LANTANA CAMARA

flower-head 3–4 in. across

hairy leaf 2–3 in. long

PENTAS LANCEOLATA
Egyptian Star Cluster

Nerium oleander may look compact in the garden centre, but remember that it will grow into a spreading shrub about 6 ft tall. If you have children or pets, also remember that it is poisonous. The flowers appear in small clusters from June until early autumn — white, pink, red and yellow varieties are available. Kohleria can grow several feet tall but the usual height is 1–2 ft. Several species are suitable for cultivation indoors, but hybrids of **K. eriantha** are usually chosen. The summer flowers are speckled inside.

Rochea coccinea is usually bought in flower during spring or summer. It is a neat plant, 1–1½ ft high, with terminal clusters of fragrant blooms in red or white. The small leaves are arranged in 4 vertical rows along each stem. **Portulaca grandiflora** can be bought as a pot plant, but it is easily raised from seed. The plants are dwarfs, growing only 4–6 in. high, and during the summer months are covered in bright single or double flowers in a wide range of colours. The common name tells you that bright light is essential.

The remarkable feature of **Lantana camara** is the darkening of each tiny tubular flower as it ages. The result is a multicoloured flower-head — the flowering season lasts from spring until late summer. This shrub with its pungent-smelling leaves can grow several feet high, but it is usually trimmed to 1–2 ft. **Pentas lanceolata** is a rare plant to find but an easy one to grow. The tubular starry flowers in white, pink, red or mauve usually appear in early winter on plants 1–1½ ft tall.

Nerium oleander La Aitana

Kohleria eriantha Success

Pentas lanceolata

● OTHER FLOWERING PLANTS continued

trumpet-shaped flower 2 in. across

narrow leaf 2 in. long

SALPIGLOSSIS SINUATA
Painted Tongue

orchid-like flower 1 in. across

ferny leaf 2 in. long

SCHIZANTHUS HYBRIDA
Poor Man's Orchid

trumpet-shaped flower 2 in. across

strap-shaped leaf 8–12 in. long

STREPTOCARPUS HYBRIDA
Cape Primrose

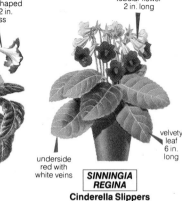

tubular flower 2 in. long

velvety leaf 6 in. long

underside red with white veins

SINNINGIA REGINA
Cinderella Slippers

multicoloured flower 6 in. across

STRELITZIA REGINAE
Bird of Paradise

paddle-shaped leaf 1 ft long on 1–2 ft leaf-stalk

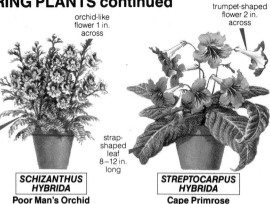

grey-green blotched with purple

fleshy erect stem 6 in. long

star-shaped flower 2–3 in across

STAPELIA VARIEGATA
Carrion Flower

Salpiglossis sinuata is a flowering pot plant which you will find in the seed catalogues rather than as a grown specimen at the garden centre. In summer the 1–2 ft stems bear large velvety blooms in a wide range of colours, the petals dark-veined and regularly arranged to form a 5-pointed star. **Schizanthus hybrida** is another colourful annual grown from seed — its flowers are unevenly lobed and yellow-eyed, giving an orchid-like appearance. Choose a compact variety (10–15 in.) such as **Hit Parade, Star Parade** or **Dwarf Bouquet**.

Illustrated here is one of the modern varieties of **Streptocarpus hybrida** — there are white, blue, purple, pink and red ones with throats which are usually clearly veined. The old favourite **Constant Nymph** (lilac with dark blue veins) is still popular. Flowering time is May to October. **Sinningia regina** may seem very similar to Streptocarpus at first glance, but the leaves are quite different in size, texture and colour. Also look at the flowers — the S. regina bloom has a prominent calyx.

Stapelia variegata is not easy to grow, and the blooms emit a foul smell. Nevertheless, some succulent enthusiasts grow this plant for the unique patterning of its large strange flowers which appear at the base of the stems during the summer. For the really keen there is the odourless **S. gigantea** (blooms 10–12 in. across). **Strelitzia reginae** is perhaps the most stunning of all indoor plants — the large bird-like flowers in red, orange and gold appear each year on mature plants. It needs space, growing 3–4 ft tall, but is nowhere near as difficult as its exotic appearance suggests.

Schizanthus hybrida

Streptocarpus Constant Nymph

Strelitzia reginae

CHAPTER 6
BONSAI

First of all, a warning. A mature and shapely bonsai is expensive, but the sight of an old and gnarled tree in a pot has led many people to regard them as ideal house plants. Be warned — they are not.

They are not house plants at all. Bonsai can have a spell indoors for four or five days at a time — place the pot in a well-lit spot and mist the leaves daily. For the rest of the time it must be kept in the garden or on a patio, to be admired through the window and provided with some protection against wind and rain.

A large number of hardy trees and shrubs can be used, but types with large leaves are not usually suitable. Conifers are favourite subjects — non-conifers include Maple, Birch, Willow, Azalea, Camellia, Hawthorn, Mountain Ash and Wisteria. It is not just a matter of keeping the plant in a pot to cramp the roots — according to the official definition a bonsai is "a tree encouraged to conform in all aspects with ordinary trees, except for its miniature size. The technique ... consists of keeping the tree confined to its pot by pinching out the top growth and pruning the roots to strike a balance between the foliage above and the roots below, and at the same time to develop a satisfactory shape."

All of this skilful pruning and training account for the high price of bonsai. The work doesn't stop when you take it home — daily watering will be necessary in summer.

Acer palmatum

Chamaecyparis pisifera

Juniperus chinensis

Pyracantha angustifolia

CHAPTER 7
WHAT THE WORDS MEAN

Flowers

Most flowers are **Self-coloured**, with just one hue covering the petals. Both **Bicoloured** and **Multicoloured** flowering plants are available.

SINGLE

The normal number of petals are present, arranged in a single row

HOSE IN HOSE

Petals are arranged so that one flower appears to be growing within another

DOUBLE

Many more petals are present than in the single form. The latin name is 'flore pleno'

SIMPLE FLOWER

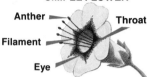

Anther
Filament
Eye
Throat

COMPOUND FLOWER

Florets
Small flowers — usually strap-shaped or ball-like

BRACT FLOWER

True flowers

Bract
Modified leaf growing near a flower which is more showy than the flower itself

SPATHE FLOWER

Spathe
Large bract surrounding the spadix

Spadix
Fleshy flower-spike bearing tiny florets

Leaves & Stems

Most leaves and stems are non-succulent. **Succulent** house plants have leaves and/or stems which are thick and fleshy.
Most house plants are **Evergreen**, retaining their leaves during the winter. The remainder are **Deciduous**.

TENDRIL
Thread-like stem or leaf which clings to any nearby support

AERIAL ROOT
Root growing out from the stem above ground level

Axil

SIMPLE LEAF
One leaf blade attached to leaf stalk

Leaf base attached to stem **Node**

COMPOUND LEAF
Two or more leaflets attached to leaf stalk

Leaf stalk

Leaflet

FROND
Leaf of a fern or a palm

OFFSET
Small plant growing at base of parent plant

GREEN LEAF
Depending upon the variety, the colour may be any shade from pale green to nearly black

VARIEGATED LEAF
Green leaf which is blotched, edged or spotted with yellow, white or cream

COLOURED LEAF
One or more colours apart from green, white or cream are distinctly present

RUNNER
Creeping stem which produces small plantlets along its length. Sometimes called a **Stolon**

Natural Habitat

EPIPHYTE
Plant which grows above ground attached to trees or rocks

AQUATIC
Plant which grows partly or wholly in water

TERRESTRIAL
Plant which grows in the soil

ROOT BALL
Matted roots plus enclosed compost within the pot

Roots

Not all the plant parts below soil level are roots. **Rhizomes** are creeping stems. **Bulbs** are short stems surrounded by rows and rows of fleshy leaves. **Tubers** and **Corms** are swollen stems which produce new plants. Some plants, such as Dahlias, produce swollen roots which are also known as **Tubers**.

House plants are grown in **Compost**, which is a mixture of materials (with or without soil) capable of supporting root growth. This 'potting compost' should not be confused with 'garden compost' made by decomposing waste plant material.

Other Terms

ALTERNATE Leaves or buds which arise first on one side of the stem and then on the other. Compare *opposite*.

ANNUAL A plant grown from seed which flowers and dies all in a single season.

APICAL At the tip of a branch.

AREOLE A small well-defined area on the stem of cacti, from which arises spines or *glochids*.

BEARDED A petal bearing a tuft or row of long hairs.

BLOOM Two meanings — either a fine powdery coating or a flower.

BOTTLE GARDEN A form of *terrarium* in which a large and heavy glass container such as a carboy is used.

BULBIL An immature small bulb formed on the stem of a plant.

BULBLET An immature small bulb formed at the base of a mature bulb.

CALYX The ring of *sepals* which covers the unopened flower bud.

CLADODE A modified stem which has taken on the form of a leaf.

CONSERVATORY A structure composed partly or entirely of glass, attached to the house and within which a large number of plants are grown and enjoyed.

COROLLA The ring of petals which is usually responsible for the main floral display.

CRESTED Cockscomb-like growth of leaves, stems or flowers. Other name — cristate.

CROWN The region where shoot and root join.

CULTIVAR Short for 'cultivated variety' — a *variety* which originated in cultivation and not in the wild.

DEAD-HEADING The removal of faded flowers.

ENTIRE LEAF An undivided and unserrated leaf.

EXOTIC Strictly speaking, a plant which is not native to the area. Popularly used for any unusual or striking specimen.

F₁ HYBRID A first generation offspring of two pure-bred *strains*.

FLOWER-SPIKE A flower-head made up of a central stalk with the flowers growing directly on it.

FORCING The process of making a plant flower before its natural time.

GENUS A group of closely-related plants containing one or more *species*.

GLOCHID A small hooked hair borne on some cacti.

GROUND COVER A plant used to provide a low-growing carpet between other plants.

GROWING POINT The tip of a stem, which is responsible for extension growth.

HARDY An indoor plant which can withstand prolonged exposure to temperatures at or below 45°F.

HYBRID A plant with parents which are genetically distinct. The parent plants may be different *cultivars*, *varieties*, *species* or *genera*.

HYDROPONICS A method of growing plants in water containing dissolved nutrients.

LEGGY Abnormally tall and spindly growth.

MICRO-CUTTING A plant produced by micropropagation — a modern technique using tiny pieces of the parent plant on a sterile nutrient jelly.

OPPOSITE Leaves or buds which are borne in pairs along the stem. Compare *alternate*.

PALMATE LEAF Five or more lobes arising from one point — hand-like.

PENDENT Hanging.

PERENNIAL A plant which can be expected to live three or more years under normal conditions.

PERFOLIATE Paired leaves which fuse around the stem.

PHYLLODE A leaf stalk expanded to look like and act like a leaf.

PINCHING OUT The removal between finger and thumb of the growing tip.

PINNATE LEAF A series of leaflets arranged on either side of a central stalk.

PIP Two meanings — the seed of some fruits (e.g Citrus) or the rootstock of some flowering plants (e.g Convallaria).

PLANT WINDOW Double window with plants grown in the space between.

SEPAL One of the divisions of the *calyx*.

SERRATE Saw-edged.

SESSILE Stalkless.

SPECIES Plants which are genetically similar and breed true to type from seed.

SPORE The reproductive cell of non-flowering plants, such as Ferns.

SPORT A plant which shows a marked and inheritable change from its parent — a mutation.

STANDARD Two meanings — the large upper petal of some flowers or a plant with a tall bare stem and a terminal head of leaves.

STRAIN A selection of a *variety*, *cultivar* or *species* which is raised from seed.

TAP ROOT A strong root, sometimes swollen, which grows vertically into the soil or compost.

TENDER An indoor plant which suffers if kept at below 60°F for a prolonged period.

TERRARIUM A partly or entirely closed glass container used to house a collection of indoor plants.

VARIETY Strictly speaking, a naturally-occurring variation of a *species* — popularly used for true varieties and *cultivars*.

WHORL Leaves, petals or branches arranged in a ring.

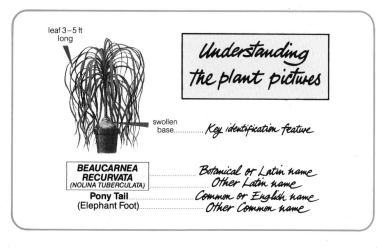

leaf 3–5 ft long

swollen base............ *Key identification feature*

Understanding the plant pictures

BEAUCARNEA RECURVATA (NOLINA TUBERCULATA) .... *Botanical or Latin name / Other Latin name*
Pony Tail (Elephant Foot) .... *Common or English name / Other Common name*

CHAPTER 8

INDEX

D

page

E